LEADER SHIP THAT LIFTS OTHERS

Turtle Publishing

First published by Turtle Publishing 2026

Cover & Illustrations by Turtle Publishing

Turtle Publishing

turtlepublishing.com.au

A Personal Note of Gratitude

To every workshop participant and client who has walked this journey with me: thank you. It has been an extraordinary privilege to work alongside you, to witness your courage, your growth, and your commitment to showing up and leading with heart.

In these challenging times, leadership is not just about direction; it's about elevation. It's about lifting others so they can grow both personally and professionally not only to become the best version of themselves but also to understand the ripple effect of their impact on those around them. Your willingness to lean in, reflect deeply, and lead with intention have inspired this book.

To my beloved husband, Mark, and our beautiful daughters, Jacinta and Kascia, your unwavering love and commitment are the foundation of everything I do. Thank you for your patience, your encouragement, and your belief in me.

A special thank you to Dr Ross James, whose wisdom and insight have once again brought this book to life with clarity and purpose. I am deeply grateful.

To Kathy Shanks and her incredible publishing team, thank you for your professionalism and care in shaping this work.

I also want to acknowledge the remarkable individuals who have been instrumental to me personally during the writing of this book: Dr Shaun Ridley, Dee Roche, Michael Burgess, Storm Dawson, Wendy Worth, and last but never least, Deanna Campisi. Your leadership, wisdom, and encouragement have lifted me so that I can continue to lift others.

With heartfelt thanks,
Dr. Nancy Pavisich

Dr Nancy Bonfiglio-Pavisich is a consultant specialising in leadership, management, and communication. She is the Director of Reframe WA Consulting and lives by the motto *review, renew, and regenerate.* Nancy is a passionate educator and facilitator who works with individuals, teams, and organisations to develop their respective leadership, management, and communication capacities.

Using evidence-based research, including neuroscience, coupled with mentoring and coaching, Nancy provides individual consultations, creates bespoke programs, facilitates workshops, and speaks publicly to support all stakeholders' personal and professional growth.

As a multi-award winner, Nancy has received an ACEL New Voice Scholarship Award (2020) and has been recognised with a Certificate of Excellence in Educational Leadership (2021) in Western Australia (ACELWA). Nancy's research has also seen her awarded A Western Australian Institute for Educational Research Award for Mentoring (2022), ACEL Fellowship Award (2022), and the Coaching Innovation Excellence Award (2025) by Corporate Vision.

Leadership That Lifts Others

Leadership isn't something we do alone. It's something we do with and for others. It's not about titles or authority. It's about how we show up in the spaces we share with our teams – every day. In this third book of the *Show Up and Lead* series, which is dedicated to exploring the essence of leadership and communication, we turn our attention outward. We explore what it means to lead in a way that builds trust, strengthens relationships, and creates the kind of workplace where people are seen, supported, and inspired to do their best work.

Our journey begins with trust, the bedrock of leadership. Trust is not a happy accident, but a deliberate construction. It's the cornerstone of our leadership, providing a secure and confident environment for our teams. This trust is built through our presence, consistency, and the courage to be authentic. When we show up emotionally – not just physically – we send a powerful message: "I'm here and I care".

We also examine the distinction between enabling and empowering. Enabling often involves doing things for others that they can do for themselves which keeps them dependent on us. Empowering, on the other hand, consists of providing the necessary resources, support, and guidance to enable others to grow and succeed. As leaders, we have the power to empower, to enable others to reach their full potential and feel capable in their roles.

Reality testing helps us stay grounded, especially when emotions run high. Social responsibility, which is a key aspect of effective leadership, reminds us that leadership is about more than individual success. It's about contributing to something bigger. It's about understanding the impact of our decisions and actions on the broader community and making choices that benefit not only our team but also the organisation and society as a whole.

Respecting the balance between knowledge and experience is an additional consideration to lifting others as we lead. We examine the mindset and skill set that enable us to lead others effectively. It's not only about what we know. It's about how we value what others bring. Knowledge and experience both matter, and great leaders know how to draw from both.

Communication matters too – not only what we say but also how we listen, how we clarify, and how we respond when things get tough. It's a cornerstone of effective leadership. And yes, social responsibility and healthy conflict are part of the deal. When conflict is healthy, it's not a threat – it's a sign that people care enough to speak up.

Learning about healthy conflict and team dynamics helps us create spaces where people thrive by collaborating and contributing in a community. As part of the leadership journey that lifts others, we talk about recognition and reward. Because people need to be seen; they need to know their work matters. Recognition isn't a nice-to-have. It's a powerful leadership tool. When we acknowledge effort, celebrate progress, and reward contribution, we build engagement, motivation, and momentum as well as show our team members that we value and appreciate their efforts. When we do these things with intention, we create a culture where people want to show up for the work and for one another.

My valued colleague, Dr Shaun Ridley, reminds me that two questions are essential for leaders to ask – and have answered – when working with their teams: How do you experience me as a leader? How do you experience yourself differently when you are in my presence? When we lead with presence and purpose, we don't only get results. We make something that lasts. Our leadership has the power to inspire, to motivate, and to create a lasting positive impact in the workplace.

My hope for you as you read this book, Leadership That Lifts Others, is that you recognise the true power of your presence as a leader. Visibility is no longer about being in the same room. It is about how consistently and intentionally you choose to engage. Your team needs to see you showing up in ways that matter: through frequent check-ins, purposeful face-to-face and online moments, and genuine signals that you are paying attention.

If you want to earn trust and elevate the people you lead, you must commit to being present – whether in person or on screen. Your visibility is a choice, and it is your responsibility to make it count. So, let's consider three mantras:

Be present, not passive

Be generous, not jealous

Be intentional, not incidental

Why have I chosen these mantras for this third book in the Show Up and Lead series?

The central message of this book is that leadership must lift others. Leadership is about responsibility, presence, and purpose. The three mantras reinforce this philosophy. Allow me to explain further.

Be Present, Not Passive

Leadership that lifts others emphasises the leadership quality of showing up emotionally and intellectually, not just physically. This mantra:

- Encourages active engagement in which leaders listen, support, and respond to their teams.

- Rejects avoidance or detachment, reminding leaders that growth in others begins with presence in oneself.

- Aligns with the book's call for mindful leadership, to be present as the first step towards lifting others.

Leaders must be visible and engaged to inspire trust and stimulate personal and professional growth in their team members

Be Generous, Not Jealous

This mantra speaks directly to the heart of leadership that lifts others. Leadership is about not elevating oneself but working with the collective.

- It promotes collaboration over competition, encouraging leaders to share credit and celebrate team wins.

- It challenges ego-driven leadership, replacing it with a culture of abundance and empowerment.

- It reflects that generosity is a catalyst for collective success. Leaders must *create space for others to shine*, knowing that authentic leadership is measured by the success of the people they lead.

Be Intentional, Not Incidental

Intentionality is a cornerstone of *leadership that lifts others*. This mantra:

- Urges leaders to make deliberate choices, aligning actions with values and vision.

- Rejects reactive or accidental leadership, advocating for strategic and thoughtful decision-making.

- Reinforces that growth is not accidental but is cultivated through purpose.

Leaders must *lead with clarity and purpose* to ensure their influence is meaningful and transformative.

As you step into the pages ahead, I invite you to pause and reflect on what you do as a leader, but also on how you show up as one. This is your moment to:

- **Review your presence:** Are you truly engaged in the spaces you occupy?

- **Renew your mindset:** Are you lifting others with generosity and intention?

- **Regenerate your impact:** Are your actions aligned with the legacy you wish to leave?

I always say that leadership is not about a title. It's a daily commitment to lift, to lead, and to leave something greater behind. Being the best version of yourself isn't a luxury; it's a necessity for those people you influence and inspire.

Let this book be your companion in reimagining leadership as a regenerative force – one that begins with you.

Contents

Conflict Intelligence 157

Team Dynamics: The Engine of Modern Leadership 181

Recognition and Reward – Lifting Others to Lead 199

Chapter One

Built on Trust

Trust is like a mirror. You can fix it if it is broken, but you can still see the cracks. ~ Richard Branson

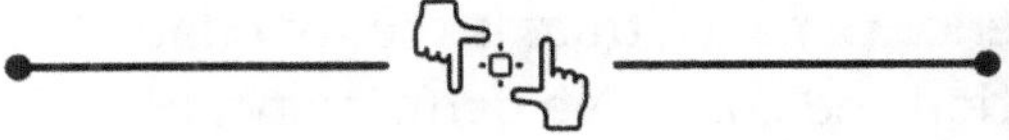

At a mid-sized tech firm facing leadership turnover and mass layoffs, the absence of transparency triggered a rapid breakdown in trust. The result? A vacuum filled with fear, gossip, and disengagement. Productivity dropped. Innovation stalled. People stopped speaking up. The company's profitability took a hit – and so did its soul.

This isn't anecdotal. Research confirms that, when trust erodes, micromanagement emerges, autonomy shrinks, and morale suffers. The culture becomes toxic, and the damage compounds. New hires leave. Long-term staff disengage. The organisation loses its edge.

Now contrast this scenario with a global consulting firm where trust was intentionally built. Leaders practised transparency, accountability, and care. Employees felt safe to take risks, share ideas, and stretch beyond their roles. The result? High engagement, low turnover, and sustained performance. Trust was not treated as a soft skill – it was a strategic asset.

———————————————————

Trust is a strategic imperative. It's the invisible architecture that holds teams, cultures, and organisations together. Yet, it's one of the most misunderstood concepts in leadership. Researchers and practitioners alike define it in various ways, but the essence remains: trust is the foundation of human connection and collective performance.

Francis Fukuyama[1] describes trust as the expectation that emerges within communities where honesty and cooperation are the norm. Amy Edmondson[2] (2003) frames it as the belief that others' future actions will align with your best interests. Brené Brown[3] reminds us that trust is built in small moments:

---

1 Fukuyama, F. (1995). *Trust: The social virtues and the creation of prosperity*. Free Press.
2 Edmondson, A. C. (2003). Speaking up in the operating room: How team leaders promote learning in interdisciplinary action teams. *Journal of Management Studies*, 40(6), 1419–1452. https://doi.org/10.1111/1467-6486.00386
3 Brown, B. (2018). *Dare to lead: Brave work. Tough conversations. Whole hearts*. Random House. ISBN 9780399592522.

through listening, keeping confidences, and showing up authentically.

In my experience working with clients, I find that trust is not one thing; it's made up of five components.

- **Reliability** – Doing what you say you'll do.
- **Integrity** – Acting ethically and honestly.
- **Competence** – Being capable and effective.
- **Benevolence** – Showing care and concern for others.
- **Vulnerability** – Willingness to take interpersonal risks.

Every high-performing team I've worked with is connected by trust. Trust is the thread that weaves individuals into a resilient, courageous collective. Without it, leadership becomes control and culture becomes collateral damage. Trust breaks down silos. It invites collaboration over competition. It reduces friction, speeds up decisions, and turns meetings into spaces for innovation rather than conflict. This isn't about being nice. It's about being real, honest, reliable and respectful.

I am reminded of Amy Edmondson's observation that growth doesn't happen in fear – it happens in safety.[2] When people are psychologically secure, they take risks, ask questions, and welcome feedback. They don't act to avoid failure but to chase possibility. And in times of change, whether it's digital transformation or organisational restructuring, trust is what keeps people grounded. It's not the absence of challenge that defines a strong culture; it's the presence of trust during challenge. As Fukuyama puts it, trust is the social capital that makes organisations work.[1]

As well, trust drives performance. Teams built on trust are more productive, more engaged, and more loyal. People care about the work as well as about one another. They are seen, heard, and valued. That energy is contagious. It fuels retention, innovation, and growth.[4]

As leaders, we must model trust. That means showing up with transparency, following through on commitments, and creating space for honest dialogue. Trust isn't built in a day. It's built in every interaction. Every decision. Every conversation.

When we lead with trust, we unlock the full potential of our people and our organisations.

---

4 Lencioni, P. (2025). *How success in 2025 depends on healthy team culture.* Growth Faculty. https://www.growthfaculty. com/blog/how-success-in-2025-depends-on-healthy-team-culture

PAUSE AND REFLECT

I invite you to think about the organisations where you have worked or are working now.

- What did trust look, feel and sound like for you at the time?

- How did the leaders exemplify trust?

- How did the employees build trust with one another?

One powerful framework for understanding trust is the Trust Triangle (Fig. 1.1). It was designed by Frances Frei and Anne Morriss at the Harvard Business School and provides a dynamic interplay of authenticity, logic, and empathy. When leaders show up with these three qualities in balance, trust isn't just possible – it is inevitable.

- **Authenticity** is the foundation. People trust leaders who are real, who speak with their own voice, own their mistakes, and lead with their values. Authenticity is not about being perfect – it's about being present.

- **Logic** builds credibility. It's not enough to care; we must also be competent. When our decisions are grounded in reason and clarity, people feel confident in our leadership.

- **Empathy** is the heartbeat of all that we do. It's what turns leadership into connection. When people are seen, heard, and valued, they lean in. Empathy doesn't dilute authority. In fact, it deepens it.

The Trust Triangle

Figure 1.1: Source: Francis Frei and Anne Morriss (2020), Begin with Trust.[5]

Trust at Work

Trust also plays a critical role in customer relationships. In a marketplace full of choices, trust is the differentiator.

---

5 Frei, F., & Morriss, A. (2020). Begin with trust: The first step to becoming a genuinely empowering leader. *Harvard Business Review,* 98(3), 112–121. https://hbr.org/2020/05/begin-with-trust

Businesses that lead with integrity and care earn three things: loyalty, repeat business, and a reputation that speaks louder than any marketing campaign. Let me share some research with you to support this assertion. Paul Zak, the founding director of the Centre for Neuroeconomics Studies, engaged in two decades of research that explored the correlation between trust and reciprocation, the interplay and synergy of both being what he described as trustworthiness.[6] His foundational studies used experimental trust games to measure the level of trust between individuals and how perceived trustworthiness influenced financial decisions. His later research focused on trust in the workplace environment, and he found that building a culture of trust is critical to successful workplaces. Zak notes that employees in organisations that foster trust tend to be more productive because they are more energised in their work. These organisations actively promote and facilitate great consultation and collaboration and do not suffer the high attrition rates of other companies.

Let's consider an example.
A standout example of an Australian company that actively builds trust in the workplace is Mantel Group, a technology consultancy specialising in digital, cloud, data, and cybersecurity.

---

6 Zak, P. J. (2017). The neuroscience of trust. *Harvard Business Review*, 95(1), 84–90.

From its inception in 2017, the Mantel Group has placed trust and people at the heart of its strategy. The founders envisioned a company culture rooted in ownership, belonging, and purpose. These three values have guided the company's rapid growth and shaped its identity. Rather than relying on traditional hierarchies, the Mantel Group operates with a flat structure by empowering employees through decentralised decision-making and peer-to-peer accountability.

The Mantel Group's commitment to trust is evident in how they engage with their team. The company conducts regular Trust Index™ surveys through Great Place To Work®, followed by in-person visits to offices across Australia and New Zealand to invite open dialogue. Leaders ask employees directly: "Is there anything you want to talk about that you didn't want to put in the survey?" It's a practice that reinforces psychological safety and transparency. The Mantel Group also embraces self-management and wholeness that is inspired by Frederic Laloux's book, *Reinventing Organisations*.[7] Every new employee receives a copy of the book, reinforcing the company's belief that trust is built when people can bring their whole selves to work.

The results speak volumes: 89 percent of Mantel Group's employees attest to the organisation being a

---

7   Laloux, F. (2014). *Reinventing organizations: A guide to creating organizations inspired by the next stage of human consciousness.* Nelson Parker.

great workplace. Notably, the company has consistently ranked highly on Australia's Best Workplaces™ list. Their trust-driven culture has resulted in increased project value, longer client engagements, and a reputation for ethical, people-first leadership.[8]

What happens when trust is absent?

Trust is the bedrock of personal relationships. Its absence can lead to significant strain because individuals may feel insecure and hesitant to share their true sentiments. A lack of genuine connection results in misunderstandings, conflicts, and a breakdown in communication.

In professional environments, the absence of trust can lead to a toxic workplace culture. Employees may feel unsupported and undervalued which decrease morale and motivation. Collaboration and teamwork can be severely impacted, as individuals may be reluctant to share ideas or take risks for fear of being judged or undermined. A lack of trust can stifle innovation and productivity, ultimately affecting the organisation's overall performance and success.

---

8   Sim, C. (n.d.). *People-first: Creating a culture of trust and ownership.* Great Place To Work Australia.

Trust is a key factor in leadership effectiveness. When employees trust their leaders, they are more likely to be engaged, committed, and productive. In the absence of trust, leadership effectiveness is compromised with employees being disengaged and less committed to the organisation's goals. Disengagement has serious consequences, including higher turnover rates and poor communication, further hindering the organisation's ability to adapt and grow.[9]

In every context – organisational, relational, societal – trust is foundational. It's not built in a vacuum. It's earned moment by moment through how we show up, how we decide, and how we care.[10] Beyond the workplace, trust is the glue that holds communities together. It underpins social cohesion, civic engagement, and the effective functioning of institutions. When trust is present, people cooperate. When it's absent, systems falter.[11]

---

9 Legood, A., van der Werff, L., Lee, A., & Den Hartog, D. (2021). A meta-analysis of the role of trust in the leadership-performance relationship. *European Journal of Work and Organizational Psychology*, 30(1), 1–22. https://doi.org/10.10 80/1359432X.2020.1819241

10 Dirks, K. T., & Skarlicki, D. P. (2004). Trust in leaders: Existing research and emerging issues. In R. M. Kramer & K. S. Cook (Eds.), *Trust and distrust in organizations: Dilemmas and approaches* (pp. 21–40). Russell Sage Foundation.

11 Fukuyama, F., & Lotterman, E. (1997). Trust: The social virtues and the creation of prosperity. *International Journal on World Peace*, 14(1), 84–87.

Leaders, you have the power to lift others through trust.

Trust is a cultural value as well as a biological catalyst for performance. A biological response occurs when the oxytocin hormone is released in the brain during moments of trust and connection. These are the moments when people are more likely to be collaborative, empathetic, and motivated. Zak[6] has rather cleverly used the word "oxytocin" as a mnemonic for eight behaviours that leaders can implement to capitalise on this response.

- **Ovation** – Recognise achievements meaningfully.

- **eXpectation** – Set clear goals and expectations.

- **Yield** – Empower employees with autonomy.

- **Transfer** – Delegate decision-making authority.

- **Openness** – Share information transparently.

- **Caring** – Show compassion and empathy.

- **Invest** – Support personal and professional growth.

- **Natural** – Be authentic and vulnerable.

Paul Zak expanded on his early research about oxytocin's role in trust and social connection by conducting new studies that examine how oxytocin influences trust and performance when both emotional and cognitive pathways are engaged.[12] Figure 1.2 summarises his findings. When oxytocin is triggered through reciprocal interactions, it fosters trust, which then drives engagement, joy and, ultimately, high performance. Purpose acts as a reinforcing agent, deepening both trust and engagement.

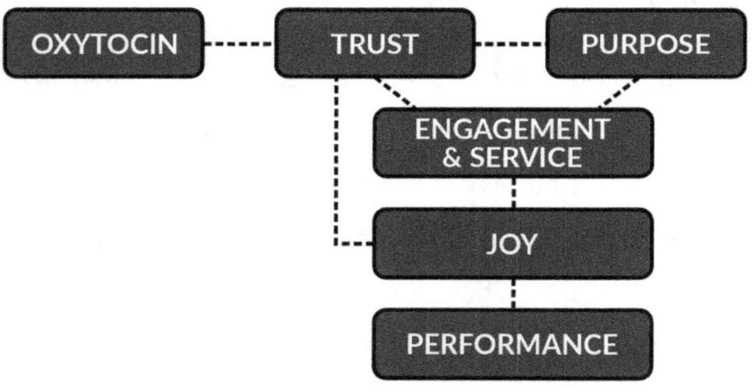

Figure 1.2: Source: Paul Zak (2023), Trust Factor.[12]

Zak's findings are echoed by Gallup's 2025 State of the Global Workplace Report,[13] which confirms that trust in leadership is a foundational driver of engagement. When employees do not trust their

---

12 Zak, P. J. (2023). *Trust factor: The science of creating high-performance companies.* HarperChristian+ORM.

13 Gallup Inc. (2025). *State of the global workplace: 2025 report.* Gallup. https://www.gallup.com/workplace/349484/state-of-the-global-workplace.aspx

leaders, they are significantly less likely to be engaged, enthusiastic, or committed to their work. Gallup further reports that manager engagement drives 70 percent of team engagement and makes the observation that declines in leadership trust in the past decade or so have contributed to a 10-year low in global employee engagement. Together, these insights underscore a powerful truth: trust is the linchpin of effective leadership. Leaders who cultivate trust through transparency, empathy, and purpose elevate individual well-being and unlock the full potential of their teams and organisations.

Trust is the currency of connection and leadership. It's not earned through titles or tenure. It's built through consistency, integrity, and presence. Leaders who embody trust and believability become anchors in their organisations. Their decisions are guided by values, not convenience, and their teams respond with loyalty, engagement, and confidence. In my book, *Show Up and Lead*,[14] I emphasise that leadership is not about being in charge. It is about being someone others can count on.

Consider the following leaders who are well known for their affinity with trust as a critical characteristic of their leadership. Equally, because they practise what

---

14 Bonfiglio-Pavisich, N. (2025). *Show up and lead: Unlock the power of self-awareness and be your best self at work.* Turtle Publishing

they preach, they are deemed believable and credible by team members and others around them.

Mary Barra, CEO of General Motors, exemplifies this principle. Her leadership is rooted in ethical clarity and accountability. By cultivating a culture where employees are encouraged to speak up, she has created psychological safety, a key ingredient in trust. When leaders listen, respond, and act with integrity, they don't just manage – they empower. Barra's approach reminds us that trust begins when leaders make space for voices beyond their own.[15]

Indra Nooyi's tenure at PepsiCo offers another powerful example. Her authentic leadership style and commitment to inclusivity built a workplace where people felt valued and heard. She didn't only talk about trust. Nooyi lived it. By investing in her people and aligning business goals with human values, Nooyi created a culture of empowerment. We know that when employees are trusted, they show up with energy, creativity, and commitment.[16]

---

15 Leadership Storybank. (2025, June 6). *Mary Barra: Leading through bold bets and cultural change.* https://www.leadershipstorybank.com/mary-barra-leading-through-bold-bets-and-cultural-change/

16 StrategyPunk. (2023, May 24). *Indra Nooyi's leadership style: Key insights and impact.* https://www.strategypunk.com/indra-nooyis-leadership-style-key-insights-and-impact

Howard Schultz of Starbucks and Arne Sorenson of Marriott International both understood that trust is built through care. Schultz prioritised employee well-being with benefits and open communication, and Sorenson led with empathy and transparency, especially in times of crisis.[17, 18]

These leaders didn't separate business from humanity. They integrated them. Their people-centric leadership created environments where trust wasn't a strategy; it was a shared experience.

As leaders, we must be present and purposeful but also precise and persuasive. We must lead with heart and with skill. We need to be intentional – not incidental – in how we show up. Today, that means being trustworthy in character as well as believable in capability. Because when people trust who you are and believe in what you do, they don't just follow – they commit. And that's where real leadership begins.

So, there you have it. Trust has long been the bedrock of meaningful leadership. It's the invisible

17   The Entrepreneur Story. (n.d.). *The success story of Starbucks and Howard Schultz: A tale of perseverance and innovation.* https://theentrepreneurstory.com/business/the-success-story-of-starbucks-and-howard-schultz-a-tale-of-perseverance-and-innovation/

18   Gallo, C. (2020, March 21). *Marriott's CEO demonstrates truly authentic leadership in a remarkably emotional video.* Forbes. https://www.forbes.com/sites/carminegallo/2020/03/21/marriotts-ceo-demonstrates-truly-authentic-leadership-in-a-remarkably-emotional-video/

thread that binds teams, strengthens relationships, and fuels engagement. When leaders show up with integrity, consistency, and care, they create environments where people are safe to contribute, collaborate, and grow. Trust is not built in grand gestures. It is earned in the quiet moments of presence: in the way we listen, respond, and lead with purpose.

As a leader who lifts others, how will you:

Be present, not passive?

Be generous, not jealous?

Be intentional, not incidental?

• • •

Takeaways

- Trust is earned moment by moment in the way we turn up.

- When trust is absent, systems falter.

- Trust is a biological catalyst for performance.

- Trust is the currency for connection.

What will you START doing?

....

....

....

....

What will you CONTINUE doing?

....

....

....

....

What will you STOP doing?

....

....

....

....

Chapter Two

Power of Presence: Leading in Real Time

Leadership is about making others better as a result of your presence and making sure that impact lasts in your absence ~ Sheryl Sandberg, former COO, Facebook

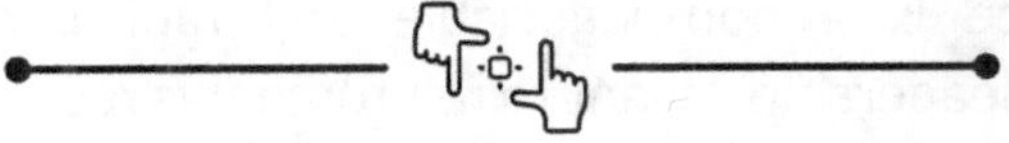

I was chatting with a client who is a senior leader in mining, responsible for five teams, each with their own direct reports. What struck me most was his unwavering commitment to being present. He said, "I don't want to just do more, I want to be more but never at the cost of showing up for my people." Despite the scale of his responsibilities, he made time to walk the sites, sit in on toolbox meetings, and check in with team leads regularly. His presence wasn't performative. It was intentional. He listened, asked questions, and made space for others to

speak. And the impact? It was palpable. Morale lifted, safety conversations deepened, and even productivity saw a boost. People felt seen, and that changed everything.

He shared that being present enabled him to catch the early signs of burnout, resolve tensions before they escalated, and build trust across all levels. "When I show up, they show up," he said. His teams began to mirror his approach: more engaged, more accountable, and more collaborative. It wasn't only about being physically there; it was about emotional availability, consistency, and genuine care. The wins were everywhere: better retention, stronger culture, and a noticeable shift in how people led one another. It reminded me that presence isn't a soft skill. It is a strategic one.

Presence is a non-negotiable and radical skill for quality leadership. I want to reinforce this requirement: presence is where people learn they are valued and respected and that their voice counts. If leaders do not actively listen in their leadership capacity, they will fail to grow trust and a deep connection with their direct reports and others.

Leaders who are consistently present within an organisation play a pivotal role in fostering trust among employees. Their visibility, accessibility, and engagement in day-to-day operations demonstrate commitment and accountability, all of which build their leadership credibility. According to a study undertaken by Mazzetti and Schaufeli and reported in the Harvard Business Review, employees are significantly more likely to trust leaders who are physically present and actively involved in their teams' work.[1] This trust creates a psychologically safe environment where employees feel valued and are more likely to share ideas, raise concerns, and collaborate openly, all of which are key ingredients for innovation and long-term success.

Mazzetti and Schaufeli found that when leaders are fully present, they lift and lead their teams and organisations by generating trust, clarity, and connection. Presence means being mentally and emotionally engaged and physically available. A present leader listens actively, observes, and responds thoughtfully. Such attentiveness helps them understand team dynamics, individual needs, and emerging challenges.[2] When employees are seen and heard, they are more likely to engage, contribute, and take ownership of their work. Presence also signals

---

1   Mazzetti, G., & Schaufeli, W. B. (2022). The impact of engaging leadership on employee engagement and team effectiveness: A longitudinal, multi-level study on the mediating role of personal and team resources. PLOS ONE, 17(6), e0269433.

2   Chen, Y., Qiang, W., & Li, F. (2024). Leader trait affective presence and safety behaviors: The role of work engagement. *Safety Science*, 169, 106339.

respect and care, which strengthens relationships and builds a culture of psychological safety.[3]

Moreover, leadership presence has a direct and significant influence on productivity and organisational growth. When leaders are present, they can provide real-time feedback, recognise achievements and swiftly address challenges, which keep teams aligned and motivated. This type of engagement translates into higher productivity, lower turnover, and a stronger organisational culture. As leaders model the behaviours they expect, they set a standard that cascades throughout the organisation to drive performance and create a resilient foundation for sustainable growth.

Research consistently shows that leaders are visibly present, whether in person or through focused real-time engagement have profound impact on trust, motivation, and workplace effectiveness. Studies published in Psychology Today demonstrate that leaders who actively "show up" through meaningful conversations, visibility and modelling values, play a critical role in shaping positive culture. Engaged employees are more likely to rate their workplace culture as good or excellent (87%) than burned-out employees (34%). Similarly, leaders who are present

---

3 Grailey, K. E., Murray, E., Reader, T., & Brett, S. J. (2021). The presence and potential impact of psychological safety in the healthcare setting: An evidence synthesis. *BMC Health Services Research*, 21(1), 1–15.

help create the psychological safety, trust and openness essential for collaboration and innovation.[4]

A client of mine - let's call him Jordan - became the regional director of a fast-growing nonprofit organisation. He made a deliberate choice to spend time on the ground with the people he led rather than staying confined to the executive office. Do not misunderstand. He navigated his daily responsibilities; however, he regularly attended team meetings when possible and participated in community outreach events. His presence wasn't just symbolic. It fostered trust, encouraged open communication, and contributed to his team being genuinely valued. Staff began to take more initiative, knowing their ideas would be heard and supported.

Professionally, Jordan's approach transformed the organisation's culture. During the first eighteen months, the organisation's culture survey revealed that employee engagement scores increased, staff turnover decreased, and innovation flourished. For Jordan, being present was something to which he aspired because of his own experience with former line managers who were frequently absent. Personally, Jordan found deeper fulfilment in his role, gaining insight into the

---

4 Teitelbaum, A. (2025, January 24). Leadership's impact on building thriving workplace cultures. *Society for Human Resource Management (SHRM)*. https://www.shrm.org/ enterprise-solutions/insights/leaderships-impact-on-building-thriving-workplace-cultures

challenges his team faced and the impact of their work. His leadership became a model of empathy and authenticity, proving that being present isn't merely good management – it's transformative.

Presence As a Leader at Work

The power of presence in the workforce refers to the ability of leaders to be fully engaged, attentive, and authentic in their interactions with employees. Presence goes beyond mere physical attendance. It involves being mentally and emotionally available, actively listening, and responding thoughtfully. When leaders show up with presence, they create an environment where employees are valued, heard, and respected.[5] That environment sustains trust and strengthens relationships, which are essential for building a cohesive and productive team. Gallup's State of The Global Workplace 2025 Report emphasises that leaders who are noted to be present and engaged are 3.4 times more likely to have highly engaged teams.[6] In fact, the data shows that 70 percent of the variance in team engagement is directly attributable to the

---

5   Hewlett, S. A. (2024). The new rules of executive presence: How leaders need to think and act now. *Harvard Business Review*, 102(1–2), 134–139.
6   Gallup. (2025). State of the global workplace: Understanding employees, informing leaders. Gallup. https://www.gallup. com/workplace/349484/state-of-the-global-workplace. aspx

manager. Equally, employees who believe their leader is present for them at work are 42 percent more likely to report high job satisfaction, and 31 percent are more likely to stay with the company for longer periods.

Understanding the importance of being present as a leader invites us to consider a framework.

The leadership presence pathway by Michael Watkins[7] is a dynamic framework that highlights the critical aspects contributing to a leader's capacity to influence. Of particular importance is the impact this pathway offers in leaving a lasting impression on the staff within an organisation. As Figure 2.1 shows, there are six stages in the leadership presence pathway: anticipation, first impressions, engagement, messaging, consolidation, and reinforcement.

---

7 Gallup. (2025). *State of the global workplace: Understanding employees, informing leaders.* Gallup. https://www.gallup.com/ workplace/349484/state-of-the-global-workplace.aspx

The Leadership Presence Pathway

Anticipation Stage
(Pre-Interaction Beliefs)

First Impressions Stage
(Initial Interaction Impressions)

Engagement Stage
(Quality of Communication)

Messaging Stage
(Content & Authenticity of Messaging)

Consolidation Stage
(Post-Interaction Influence)

Reinforcement Stage
(Follow-Up Communication)

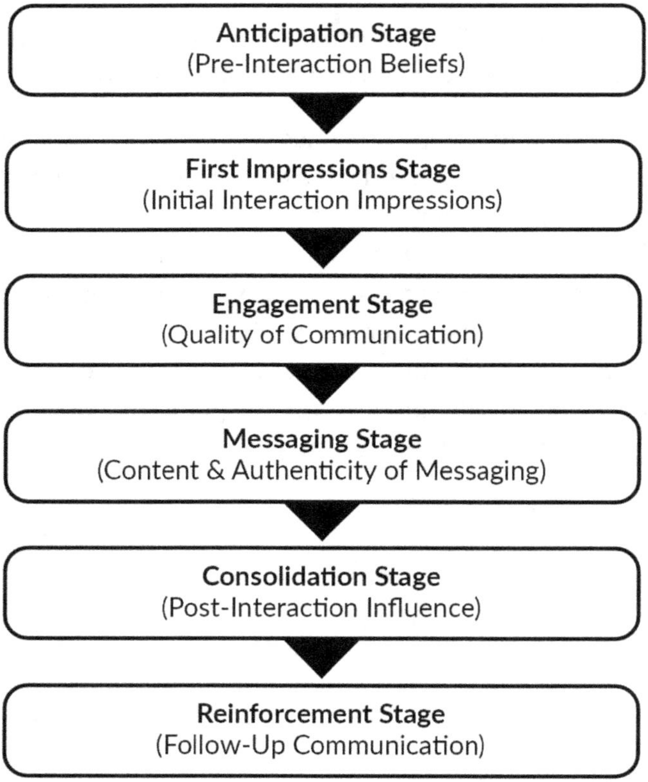

Figure 2.1: Source: Watkins (2024), The leadership presence pathway.[7]

Anticipation

The anticipation stage, occurring before any direct interaction, is shaped by what others believe or expect about a leader. Leaders have the power to influence this stage by managing their personal brand, consistently demonstrating their values in their actions and communications, and aligning it with their values and leadership identity. This empowerment allows leaders to shape their leadership narrative and take control of the anticipation stage.

As in my previous two books, *It's All About It! Evidence-based practical guide to workplace communications*[8] and *Show Up and Lead*[9], I speak of Richard Branson (founder of the Virgin Group) as a leader who works diligently to practise what he preaches. Branson's adventurous, people-first leadership style is a direct reflection of his personal brand. He's known for being approachable, bold, and values-driven, which resonates across Virgin's customer experience and employee culture. He has built Virgin's culture around trust, autonomy, and emotional safety, encouraging innovation and risk-taking even if it means making mistakes. Branson's approach includes walking around during flights to personally gather feedback from staff, reinforcing his belief in direct, respectful communication

---

8   Bonfiglio-Pavisich, N. (2024). *It's all about IT!: Evidence-based, practical guide to workplace communications.* Turtle Publishing
9   Bonfiglio-Pavisich, N. (2025). *Show up and lead: Unlock the power of self-awareness and be your best self at work.* Turtle Publishing

and employee involvement.[10] His words also match his actions. By prioritising employees before customers and shareholders, Branson has created a family-like, non-hierarchical environment that fosters loyalty, creativity, and long-term success.[11]

First Impressions

First impressions are powerful. They are those pivotal moments when a leader's presence begins to shape how others feel, connect, and engage. When leaders show up with authenticity that is expressed physically, emotionally, and energetically, they set the tone for trust, credibility, and approachability. It's not limited to appearance or words but encompasses the calmness in their voice, the empathy in their eyes, and the confidence in their posture. These subtle cues speak volumes, signalling to teams that their contributions matter and their voices are heard. The weight of these initial interactions underscores the importance of leaders' first impressions in the leadership journey.[12]

---

10 Priyansha, M. (2017). Richard Branson: 'Clients do not come first. Employees come first.' *HR Digest (online)*. https://www.thehrdigest.com/richard-branson-clients-do-not-come-first-employees-come-first/

11 Branson, R. (2008). *Business stripped bare: Adventures of a global entrepreneur*. Random House.

12 Astray, T. (2025). *Mastering first impressions at every career level: From new hire to CEO*. https://www.tatianaastray.com/mastering-the-self/2025

Engagement

Engagement in leadership is more than just being visible. It's about cultivating meaningful, sustained interactions that reinforce alignment, accountability, and shared purpose. In the medical field, for example, department heads who consistently do ward rounds with their teams, listen to concerns and respond with empathy, build a relational presence that goes far beyond administrative oversight. Their emotional and psychological availability strengthens trust and psychological safety, allowing staff to be seen, heard, and valued. Over time, such interactions deepen influence and create a culture in which leadership is both observed and felt. It's in these moments that a leader's presence becomes a powerful force for connection and inclusion, ultimately enhancing both team morale and patient care outcomes.

Messaging: Sustained Interaction

Messaging is about what we say (content) and the authenticity of our communication. I often share in my workshops that a single conversation is rarely enough to build an authentic connection. Actual leadership presence is cultivated through consistent engagement, or sustained interaction, so that leaders are not only seen and heard but also are actively seeing and hearing others. What do I mean by sustained interaction? In our day-to-day workplace routines, many things occupy our thoughts and attention, and it is easy to give people scant attention even as we say "yeah, yeah, okay". It's fogging; it's hearing but not listening. Sustained interaction is when we stop, focus, be present, and connect. Sustained interaction is authentic communication that is not relegated to inattentive responses.

The practice of sustained interaction cultivates mutual reciprocity, which strengthens psychological safety and encourages deeper learning, increased contribution, thoughtful risk-taking, and respectful challenges to the status quo. At this stage, consistency becomes key. Leaders must move beyond strong first impressions and demonstrate reliability through authentic, ongoing interactions.[13] Sustained interaction addresses conflict directly and respectfully, offering constructive and specific feedback, and showing genuine empathy and support. Consistent behaviours build credibility and deepen trust, enabling others to experience being valued and respected

A simple example of how sustained interaction helps develop leader and employee relationships is a leader who holds regular one-on-one check-ins with each team member. Over time, these consistent conversations enable the manager to gain a deeper understanding of the individual's strengths, challenges, and goals. Employees begin to feel more comfortable

---

13 Allas, T., & Schaninger, B. (2020). The boss factor: Making the world a better place through workplace relationships. *The McKinsey Quarterly Journal.*

sharing ideas and concerns, knowing they'll be heard and supported because that ongoing dialogue builds trust, strengthens rapport, and creates a more collaborative and motivated work environment.

Consolidation: Reflection

Consolidation is what happens after an interaction. Consolidation is when leaders reflect on how their behaviours, decisions, and communication affect those around them. Consolidation and reflection occur when we apply the leadership presence pathway to bridge our intention and its consequent impact. Leaders will develop deeper insights with consistent, critical self-reflection on how to adapt their communication approach to better meet the evolving needs of their teams. At the same time, followers begin to reflect on their experiences with their leaders, evaluating whether their leaders' actions align with their stated values and commitments. These reflections shape long-term perceptions of integrity, reliability, and authenticity. Leaders who actively invite feedback and demonstrate self-awareness reinforce their presence, which builds trust and strengthens relationships through transparency and growth.[14]

---

14 Edmondson, A. C. (2003). Speaking up in the operating room: How team leaders promote learning in interdisciplinary action teams. *Journal of Management Studies*, 40(6), 1419–1452.

Reinforcement

The final stage is about growth and adaptability. Leaders must adapt their presence as workplace or organisational contexts evolve – whether through new roles, teams, or challenges. It requires continuous learning, emotional agility, and the ability to re-engage with authenticity. For instance, in a new team, a leader might need to be more open and communicative to establish trust. In this stage, presence becomes a living practice of leadership maturity.

PAUSE AND REFLECT

Self-Reflection

1. How did my presence influence the tone of today's interaction?

2. Did my actions today align with my values and intentions?

3. What emotional cues did I convey? How might they have been received?

4. Where did I show up authentically? What do I need to do more or less of to show up authentically?

Relational Reflection

1. How well did I listen and respond to the needs of the team I lead?

2. Did I create space for others to be seen, heard, and valued?

3. What feedback have I received? How can I use it to grow?

4. Am I consistently reinforcing trust and psychological safety?

Strategic Reflection

1. What patterns are emerging in how I engage with others?

2. How am I adapting my leadership presence to meet evolving team dynamics?

3. What impact am I having on team morale, learning, and contribution?

4. How can I better model the behaviours I want to see in others?

Why Presence Matters

Presence is one of the most powerful gifts we can offer in any relationship. It's not about having all the answers; it's about showing up with our full attention, our whole heart, and our full humanity. In a world that moves fast and often values productivity over connection, being present is a radical act of leadership that declares "I see you, I hear you, and you matter". In that moment of connection, trust begins to grow.

The power of leadership presence is significant because it has a profound impact on the quality of interactions and relationships in both personal and professional settings. When leaders and individuals are fully present, they create an environment of trust, respect, and engagement. Presence allows for deeper connections because people feel heard, valued, and understood. In the workplace, it can lead to higher levels of collaboration, innovation, and overall job satisfaction.

I often hear, "Our leaders are never around, they are absent". I'm reminded of an event I attended a long time ago. As we chatted about how to grow and develop people, an individual from the group shouted out "presence and proximity". You cannot connect with people if you are not around. A true point. So, I designed a quadrant to capture that comment in a little more detail (Fig. 2.2).

Presence and Proximity

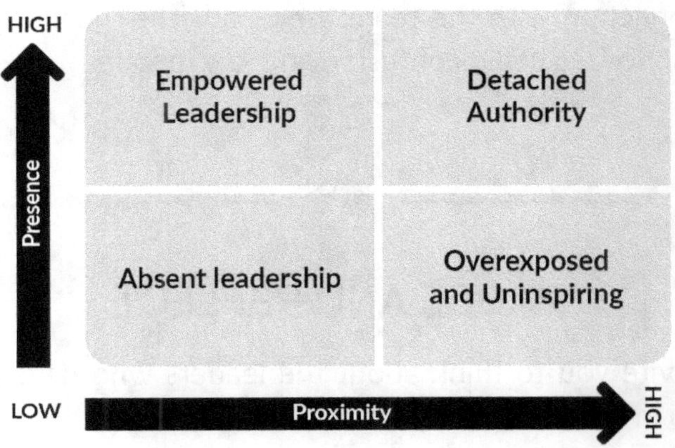

Figure 2.2: Source: N. Bonfiglio-Pavisich, © (2025).

High Presence and High Proximity is the ideal zone for leaders where they are physically and relationally connected to their teams and actively engaged. Leaders in this space boost trust, motivation and create conditions for strong team dynamics.

The *High Presence and Low Proximity* zone highlights empowered leadership. Leaders in this zone are visible and rely on the knowledge, skills and understandings of employees to make appropriate decisions in their respective teams.

Leaders in the *Low Presence and High Proximity* zone are relational but lack meaningful engagement. Their influence may be overexposed and uninspiring.

Leaders in the *Low Presence and Low Proximity* zone are physically and emotionally absent. They lack connection with the team they lead. Their leadership absence results in confusion and low morale.

PAUSE AND REFLECT

I invite you to think about the leaders who have led you in the past.

- Where would you place them on this quadrant?

- What reasons would you give?

- Where do you fit on the Presence versus Proximity Quadrant?

When leaders are present, they are more attuned to the nuances of situations and the perspectives of their team members. Their insights and awareness enable them to make more informed and thoughtful decisions and to problem-solve by addressing issues proactively and effectively. By being present, leaders can navigate challenges with clarity and confidence, inspiring their teams to do the same, thereby improving problem-solving skills and team dynamics.[15]

Furthermore, the power of presence strengthens a positive and supportive work culture. When employees believe their leaders are genuinely engaged and invested in their well-being, they are more likely to be motivated and committed to their work.[16] In this way, leadership presence can produce increased productivity, reduced turnover, and a stronger sense of community within the organisation. Presence also sets a positive example, encouraging employees to adopt similar behaviours and attitudes, thereby creating a more enjoyable and productive workplace.

When facilitating workshops, I remind participants that the power of presence is about creating meaningful and impactful interactions. It serves to build a foundation of trust and respect, which is essential for the growth and well-being of individuals, teams and organisations. By cultivating presence, leaders can drive positive change and achieve lasting success for their teams, their organisation and, not least, for themselves.

---

15 Jeffrey, B., Weddle, B., Brassey, J., & Thaker, S. (2025). Thriving workplaces: How employers can improve productivity and change lives. *The McKinsey Quarterly Journal.*
16 Hewlett, S. A., & Ashford, R. (2014). *Executive presence.* HarperCollins.

Why Does Presence Matter for Leaders?

In the workplace, presence is what turns leaders into mentors and colleagues into collaborators. Leaders change culture when they take the time to listen without distraction, ask questions that invite reflection, and sit with discomfort rather than rushing to fix it. The leader-managers I work with usually believe they must fix the problems brought to them by staff. I suggest to them that they sit with the discomfort of the problem but work through it in a coaching conversation and let their staff do the talking. All the leader-manager needs to do is listen and work through the solutions offered by staff.

People begin to recognise that they are valued not just for what they do but for who they are. That's when engagement deepens, creativity flourishes, and resilience grows.[15]

For leaders, living the power of presence means consistently demonstrating these qualities in their daily interactions. It involves making a conscious effort to be present in meetings, one-on-one conversations, and even in casual encounters. Leaders who practise presence are attentive to the needs and concerns of their team members and provide support and guidance when needed. By being fully engaged, they can better understand the dynamics of their team and address issues proactively, leading to a more harmonious and efficient workplace.

An example of this is evident in the following story with details and names changed to protect the privacy of my client.

At Willow Creek Aged Care, staff were overwhelmed, and morale was low. Helen, the manager, spent most of her time in her office, unaware of the daily struggles her team faced.

One day, she changed course. Helen began walking the facilities, listening to staff and engaging with residents. She noticed small issues before they became big problems and made decisions based on real insights. Her presence transformed the culture. Staff felt supported, residents felt cared for, and the team began working together with renewed energy. Helen's simple act of being present made all the difference.

The power of presence also extends to how leaders handle challenges and opportunities. Leaders who are present are more likely to make informed and thoughtful decisions because they are attuned to the nuances of situations and the perspectives of their team. Their presence allows them to navigate complex issues with clarity and confidence, inspiring their team to do the same. Moreover, leaders who embody presence set a positive example for their employees, encouraging them to adopt similar behaviours and attitudes.[13]

Ultimately, the power of presence can transform the workplace by creating a culture of engagement, trust and collaboration. When leaders are present, they foster an environment where employees are empowered to contribute their best work. The widespread benefits include higher levels of job satisfaction, increased productivity, and a stronger sense of community within the organisation. By making presence a lived experience, leaders can drive meaningful change and achieve lasting success for their teams and their organisations.

Who Are Examples of People with Presence?

Barack Obama

Former US President Barack Obama is widely admired for his composure, gravitas, and exceptional communication skills. His presence is characterised by his calm demeanour, thoughtful speech, and ability to inspire. During times of crisis, such as the economic recession and various international challenges, Obama's leadership showcased his ability to remain poised and decisive. His presence has left a lasting impact on both national and global stages.

Sheryl Sandberg

Sheryl Sandberg, the Chief Operating Officer of Facebook and author of *Lean In*,[17] is a role model for many women in leadership positions. Her presence is characterised by her confidence, clarity, and

---

17 Sandberg, S. (2015). *Lean in.* W H Allen

unwavering commitment to gender equality worldwide. Sandberg's ability to articulate her vision and advocate for women's empowerment has made her a prominent and respected leader. Her presence encourages others to strive for excellence and break down barriers in their professional lives.

Rosie Batty

As a domestic violence campaigner and 2015 Australian of the Year, Rosie Batty has used her personal tragedy to advocate for change and support for victims of domestic violence. Her presence is marked by her courage, authenticity, and an unwavering dedication to raising awareness and driving policy reform.

PAUSE AND REFLECT

Having read about presence so far and learned about leaders who exemplify presence, what do you need to do more or less of as you lift the people you lead?

Let's Think About Presence in Our Work Conversations

Presence in conversation is more than a courtesy: it's actually a leadership discipline. When we engage with stakeholders, whether they are team members, clients, board members, or community partners, our ability to be fully present signals respect, attentiveness, and integrity. It's easy to underestimate the power of eye contact, active listening, and undivided attention, but these are the very behaviours that build trust and credibility. In a distracted world, presence is rare and is, therefore, deeply valued.

Some people listen only to prepare for their response; they're thinking about what they want to say. That's not being present. Being present means listening to understand by tuning into the emotional tone of the conversation, not just the words being spoken. When leaders exhibit emotional and psychological presence, they create a space for others to speak honestly, share their concerns, and offer ideas. This type of engagement stimulates psychological safety, which research findings reveal is essential for innovation, collaboration, and long-term performance.[13]

Stakeholders are looking for more than answers: they're looking for connection. Whether it's a frontline employee seeking clarity, a client navigating uncertainty, or a board member weighing strategic decisions, presence communicates commitment.

Bravo,[18] in his contribution to Forbes Coaches Council Post, notes that leaders who are present in conversations are more likely to inspire loyalty, reduce conflict, and drive alignment. Presence is the bridge between intention and impact. Ultimately, being present is about showing up with purpose. It's about recognising that every conversation is an opportunity to lead, to learn, and to build trust. When we are physically, emotionally, and psychologically present, we do more than communicate: we connect. When we're connected, we can create the conditions for meaningful progress, a shared vision, and enduring success.

What Else Might We Consider to Cultivate Presence in the Workplace?

Active Listening

One of the most powerful ways to demonstrate presence is through active listening. Turn your listening skills to active by giving the speaker your full attention, maintaining eye contact, and responding thoughtfully

---

18 Bravo, A. (2025, April 9). 7 trust-building behaviors that set great leaders apart. *Forbes.* https://www.forbes.com/councils/forbescoachescouncil/2025/04/09/7-trust-building-behaviors-that-set-great-leaders-apart/

and respectfully. Avoid interrupting or thinking about your response while the other person is speaking. By truly listening, you show that you value and respect their knowledge, experience and insights.

Authenticity

Being authentic means being true to yourself and your values. When you are genuine in your interactions, people are more likely to trust and connect with you. Share your thoughts and emotions openly and encourage others to do the same. Authenticity fosters deeper connections and builds trust.

Empathy

Empathy involves understanding and sharing the feelings of others. Practise putting on your 'others' shoes and consider the situation from their perspectives. Show compassion and support and be responsive to their needs. Empathy enables you connect with others on a deeper level and enhances your presence as a leader.

Continuous Learning

Stay curious and committed to personal and professional growth. Seek feedback from others and be open to learning from your experiences. By continuously improving your skills and knowledge, you can better support and lead your team.

Body Language

Nonverbal communication plays a significant role in presence. Pay attention to your body language such as maintaining eye contact, using open gestures, and having a confident posture. Positive body language reinforces your verbal messages and enables you to connect with others more effectively.

The Benefits of Being Present

When leaders are fully present, their ability to manage people becomes more intuitive and responsive. For instance, a manager who regularly engages with their team can detect subtle shifts in morale or behaviour (such as an employee who is typically enthusiastic becoming withdrawn) and addresses concerns before they escalate. A proactive presence sustains a supportive environment where individuals are valued and understood. By consistently checking in, asking meaningful questions, and following through on concerns, leaders validate their team members' experiences and encourage personal growth, which strengthens overall team cohesion and retention.

From a productivity standpoint, present leaders are better equipped to align goals, remove barriers, and maintain momentum. Consider a project leader who holds weekly strategy sessions, listens actively to feedback, and adjusts timelines based on team input. This level of attentiveness ensures that everyone remains focused and clear on priorities, which reduces confusion and improves execution. When communication is consistent and expectations are transparent, teams experience fewer errors and more efficient workflows. Employees who know their leader is engaged and accessible are more likely to stay motivated, take initiative, and remain accountable.

Presence also plays a direct role in driving profitability. For example, a CEO who regularly interacts with frontline staff and clients gains real-time insights that inform better decision-making. This visibility builds trust with stakeholders and enhances the organisation's reputation. Engaged teams, led by present leaders, tend to innovate more and deliver higher-quality outcomes, all of which contribute to long-term value. In this way, presence becomes a strategic asset because it lifts individuals, aligns efforts, and sustains success across people, productivity, and profits.

Leadership presence is more than a trait – it's a call to action. It invites leaders to **be present, not passive**, by engaging actively and attentively with their teams, thereby creating space for growth, contribution, and confidence. It challenges leaders to **be generous, not jealous**, celebrating the success of others and fostering a culture of collaboration over competition. It urges leaders to **be intentional, not incidental**, aligning their actions with purpose to drive clarity, momentum, and impact. When leaders embody these mantras, they don't merely lead – they elevate. Presence becomes a force for empowerment, transforming workplaces into environments where people thrive, productivity flows, and purpose is shared. Now is the time to lead with presence deliberately, generously, and wholeheartedly.

• • •

Takeaways

- First impressions set the emotional tone.

- Sustained interaction builds trust and engagement.

- Reflection reinforces integrity and growth.

What will you START doing?

What will you CONTINUE doing?

What will you STOP doing?

Chapter Three

Empowerment and Enablement: Two Sides of Leadership

The function of leadership is to produce more leaders, not more followers. ~ Ralph Nader

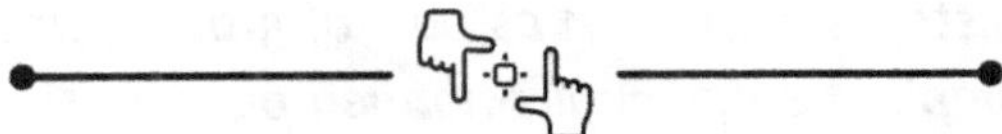

Ingvar Kamprad (the founder of IKEA, the multinational retail company) once said, "If there is such a thing as good leadership, it is to give a good example."[1] And he lived it every day. Despite being one of the wealthiest men in the world, Kamprad famously drove an old Volvo, flew

---

1 Lemayian, D. (2024, January 27). *The testament of a furniture dealer: IKEA's timeless handbook on values and the visionary legacy of Ingvar Kamprad.* https://davidlemayian.com/blog/2024/01/27/ikea/

economy class, and took public transport, even as the founder of a global empire. His frugality wasn't merely personal; it was a message to his employees: we're all in this together. He didn't just talk about values like humility and simplicity; he modelled them. This created a culture where employees felt respected and inspired. They saw that leadership wasn't about status; it was about service. Kamprad's example encouraged IKEA staff to take pride in their work, focus on customer needs, and find creative solutions without excess. Productivity rose not because of pressure, but because of shared purpose.

Kamprad believed deeply in empowering people. He once said, "The fear of making mistakes is the root of bureaucracy and the enemy of development."[2] At IKEA, he gave young, inexperienced employees real responsibility trusting them to lead, innovate, and learn through doing. This wasn't reckless; it was intentional. Kamprad saw potential where others saw risk. He created a culture where mistakes were seen as part of growth, not failure. One example: he personally handed out Christmas gifts to thousands of employees, reinforcing that every person mattered. This kind of leadership built loyalty, boosted morale, and encouraged initiative. Employees felt safe to experiment, speak up, and take ownership. The result? A workforce that was engaged, agile, and deeply aligned with IKEA's mission to serve many. Kamprad's legacy lives

---

2 Dudovskiy, J. (2022, August 14). *IKEA leadership: Effective application of leading by example.* Research-Methodology. https://research-methodology.net/ikea-leadership-effective-application-leading-example/

on in a company where empowerment isn't a buzzword. It's a way of life.

* * *

As leaders, we often ask ourselves: "Do I empower the people I work with, or do I enable them?" It's a subtle distinction, yet one that profoundly shapes how we lead, how others grow, and how our organisation evolves. You might be wondering, *What's the difference?* These terms are frequently used interchangeably, but they represent distinct leadership philosophies. Understanding their differences is essential for cultivating a workplace culture that is both high performing and deeply human.

Trayton Vance, CEO of Coaching Focus Ltd, in an interview for Consultant Magazine captures the differences beautifully: empowerment in the workplace gives power and enablement gives means.[3]

Empowerment is about *agency*. It's the practice of granting autonomy, authority, and trust. Empowering leaders invites initiative, decision-making, and

---

3 Vance, T. (2025, July 3). Trayton Vance, CEO and Founder, Coaching Focus Ltd. *Consultant Magazine.* https:// consultantmagazine.co/interview/trayton-vance-ceo-and- founder-coaching-focus-ltd-1/

ownership. According to Kirkman et al.,[4] empowerment cultivates a sense of accountability and personal investment in outcomes. It is leadership that says, "I trust you to lead from where you are".

Enablement, by contrast, is about creating the *conditions for success*. It involves equipping individuals with the tools, resources, training, and support they need to perform. Enablement is the act of removing barriers and ensuring that people have what they need to thrive. As Gupta notes, when we enable leaders, we focus on capacity building.[5] Capacity building is important because it provides the groundwork for others to flourish.

I emphasise to clients the distinction between empowerment and enablement, highlighting that the concepts can support each other. For example, empowerment without enablement in the workplace can cause employees to perceive themselves as unsupported. However, an emphasis on enablement without empowerment can result in employees feeling a lack of control in their day-to-day work. Together, empowerment and enablement can form a

---

4 Kirkman, B., Chen, G., & Mathieu, J. (2020). Improving employee performance by developing empowering leaders & companies. *Behavioral Science & Policy*, 6(1), 23–36. https://link.springer.com/chapter/10.1007/978-3-319-94259-9_2
5 Gupta, A. (2024). Employee enablement. In F*ostering open source culture: Increase innovation and deliver faster with open source* (pp. 283–303). Berkeley, CA: Apress. https://link.springer.com/chapter/10.1007/979-8-8688-0977-4_7

dynamic leadership strategy, one that nurtures both competence and confidence.

Consider a client of mine, Jim (a pseudonym). Jim has two line managers because his role and responsibilities lean into two divisions within the company. The first line manager, who has an empowerment philosophy, invites Jim to use his knowledge, skills, and understanding to engage with any task. Jim is autonomous in his work and in the relevant decisions that need to be made. The first line manager is supportive, believes empowerment is the key to productivity and company success. That is why, should Jim get stuck or need to talk through an idea, he is encouraged to think outside the box and come to the answer himself. Jim is empowered.

The second line manager is an enabler who tends to control Jim. He wants Jim to consult with him before making any decision and explain the reasoning behind that decision. Jim also needs to be explicit in his communication to ensure the task is completed according to the second line manager's preferred method. Consequently, Jim spends a lot of his time going backwards and forwards before a decision is made. Jim struggles with this form of management because he no longer is confident to make a decision on his own.

Empowerment Versus Enablement

When coaching company and local government executives, I emphasise that today's dynamic and evolving workplaces require leaders to foster both individual empowerment and collective enablement. People need the agency to act, contribute and lead, while teams need the structures, support and conditions that allow them to thrive together. The partnership of empowerment and enablement is foundational to building workplaces capable of adapting, innovating and sustaining performance over time. They are essential if we are to lift others as we lead.

Let's Consider Some Theoretical Frameworks

Empowerment theory, as explained by Thomas and Velthouse,[6] is a framework for understanding how individuals and communities gain control over their lives, influence decisions, and act on what matters to them. The application of empowerment theory enables us to consider the psychological, social, and structural dimensions of leadership instead of taking

---

6 Thomas, K. W., & Velthouse, B. A. (1990). Cognitive elements of empowerment: An "interpretive" model of intrinsic task motivation. *Academy of Management Review*, 15(4), 666–681.

solely managerial actions. The theory itself provokes our thinking and invites us to ask:

- Are we cultivating self-efficacy?

- Are we encouraging participation?

- Are we enabling transformative change?

As leaders, our role is to guide as well as create space. The quality of the space is critical for others to grow, to lead, and to shape the future. Leaning into our internal cognitive states contributes to empowerment. These cognitive states have four key dimensions: meaning, competence, self-determination, and impact.

Meaning

When we lead to lift others, we create conditions that have meaning. Often, the degree to which an experience is meaningful is aligned with our motivation. The alignment between an individual's work and their personal values creates opportunities for meaning and, of course, motivation. We learn a lot about this from the work of Wan Fauzia Yusoff and her colleagues who investigated a theory of work motivation originally put forward in the 1950s and 1960s by Frederick Herzberg, a psychologist who specialised in business management.

Herzberg's Two Factors Theory related to how workers' personal feelings towards their working environments influenced their workplace attitudes and level of performance. The two factors were motivation or intrinsic factors that increase worker job satisfaction and hygiene or extrinsic factors to prevent dissatisfaction.

But it became clear that the Two Factors Theory is no longer practical for explaining or prompting motivation in today's workplace environments. Figure 3.1 depicts the research findings of Yusoff and her colleagues that workers' preferences for being motivated is changing. Their preferences relate to meaningful work, for achievement, personal growth and recognition. If those preferences are met, they are more likely to be satisfied and motivated.[7]

Motivation Model of Work Performance

Figure 3.1: Source: Yusoff et al. (2013), Herzberg's Two Factors Theory on work motivation.[7]

---

7   Yusoff, W. F. W., Kian, T. S., & Idris, M. T. M. (2013). Herzberg's two factors theory on work motivation: Does it work for today's environment? *Global Journal of Commerce and Management*, 2(5), 18–22.

Competence

The concept of identity at work is shaped by comfort, competence, and confidence. Competence and confidence, particularly, were highlighted in an influential essay by Charles H. Christiansen.[8] The essay is Christiansen's exploration of how an individual's job, that is, the roles and tasks performed, serves as a primary means through which they develop and express their personal identities. Christiansen emphasises:

- Competence in performing tasks contributes to identity formation.

- Coherence and well-being are outcomes of realising an acceptable identity.

- Identity provides a framework for goal setting, motivation, and meaning-making.

If we are to lift others as we lead, growing people's competence is critical to personal and professional growth. When individuals perceive themselves as competent, that is, when they believe they can perform the task effectively, they have greater confidence. Matthews[9] reported on the work of military psychologist, Patrick J. Sweeney, a US Army

---

8   Christiansen, C. H. (1999). Defining lives: Occupation as identity: An essay on competence, coherence, and the creation of meaning. *The American Journal of Occupational Therapy*, 53(6), 547–558.

9   Matthews, M. D. (2016). The 3c's of trust. *Psychology Today.* https://www.psychologytoday.com/au/blog/head-strong/201605/the-3-cs-of-trust

colonel who undertook field research during the 2003 Iraq War. Sweeney discovered that three traits were critical to a soldier's trust in their leaders: competency, character, and caring. Sweeney found that soldiers led by officers who exemplified these traits ultimately were more effective. In reviewing Sweeney's work, Matthews concluded that being competent, of great character, and caring are all necessary components, but none alone were sufficient for quality leadership.

Self-Determination

Being autonomous at work, that is, being able to use the knowledge, skills, and understandings for which we were hired, is an essential element of self-determination. In my experience, the more employees perceive themselves as competent and confident in using their skills, the better equipped they are to make the relevant decisions required at work. The impact of self-determination extends beyond being given authority and responsibility: it is about how their work can influence organisational outcomes.[10] Deci and

---

10 Parker, L. E., & Price, R. H. (1994). Empowered managers and empowered workers: The effects of managerial support and managerial perceived control on workers' sense of control over decision making. *Journal of Human Relations*, 47(8), 911–928.

Ryan[11] (1985) believe it is critical for leaders to shift their perspective from external rewards and control to internal motivation and psychological well-being.

The Self-Determination Theory (Fig. 3.2) centres on three core psychological needs: autonomy, competence, and relatedness. When leaders intentionally nurture these needs, they move beyond surface-level empowerment. They create environments where individuals are genuinely capable, connected, and free to act with purpose. This is the space where true engagement and ownership flourish, leading to sustained performance and well-being across teams.

The Self-Determination Theory

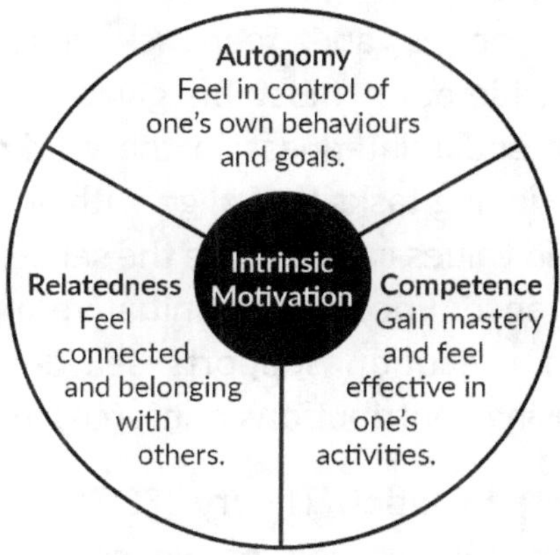

Figure 3.2: Source: N. Bonfiglio-Pavisich, © (2025).

---

11 Deci, E. L., & Ryan, R. M. (1985). *Intrinsic motivation and self-determination in human behavior.* Springer. https://doi.org/10.1007/978-1-4899-2271-7

Leaders who support autonomy or self-determination are more likely to create environments where people thrive by allowing employees to make decisions, build their competence through feedback and development opportunities, and foster relatedness by cultivating trust and collaboration. This approach enhances both individual performance and contributes to a more resilient and innovative organisational culture.

True empowerment is not merely about delegating tasks or granting decision-making power; it's about cultivating an environment where employees are empowered. Leaders must therefore focus on enhancing these psychological states through meaningful work, skill development, autonomy support, and feedback that reinforces impact. Consideration must be given to autonomy, competence and relatedness in the workplace.[11] For example, assigning tasks that align with an employee's strengths and values can increase the sense of meaning and competence. Encouraging initiative and allowing flexibility in execution supports self-determination, and recognising contributions reinforces impact.

Self-Determination Theory (SDT) in action is a roadmap for empowering employees in ways that sustain motivation and engagement over time. Let's consider the Meaningful Work and Performance Model designed by van Wingerden and van der Stoep to summarise their research findings on teachers in an educational setting (Fig.3.3).[12] The model highlights the indirect effect that meaningful work has on performance.

Meaningful Work and Performance Model

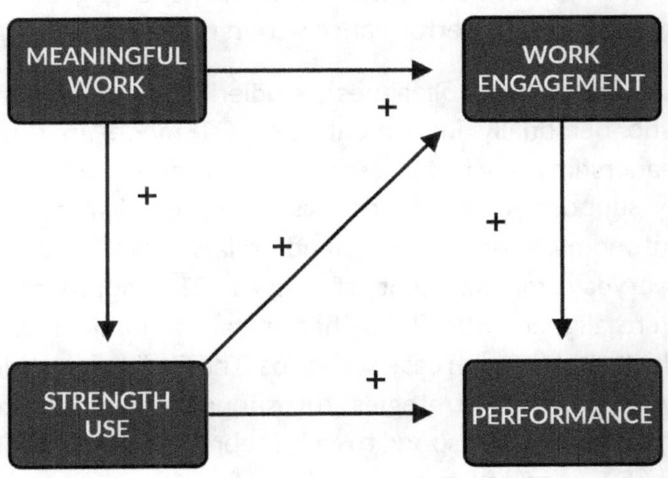

Figure 3.3: Source: van Wingerden and van der Stoep (2018), The motivational potential of meaningful work.[12]

When we feel we are using our strengths in meaningful work, our self-confidence and competence are validated, which leads to better engagement with work tasks. The model shows that meaningful

---

12 van Wingerden, J., & van der Stoep, J. (2018). The motivational potential of meaningful work: Relationships with strengths use, work engagement, and performance. *PLOS ONE*, 13(6). https://doi.org/10.1371/JOURNAL.PONE.0197599.

work can be connected to performance in multiple ways. For example, in the context of this research on teachers, when they perceived their work as having value, they engaged with interconnected processes that resulted in a positive impact on their performance. The application to leaders is to move beyond surface-level empowerment and generate deeper engagement, ownership, and performance within their teams.

Forner and colleagues[13] studied fifty-one leaders who personally implement the SDT model in their leadership practices. Leaders operationalised SDT by supporting employees' basic psychological needs: autonomy, competence, and relatedness through everyday management strategies. The approaches were aligned with SDT's theoretical foundations and illustrated through case scenarios. The findings provide new, practical strategies for supporting workplace motivation and respond to calls for broader exploration of SDT-informed managerial behaviours.

---

13 Forner, V. W., Jones, M., Berry, Y., & Eidenfalk, J. (2021). Motivating workers: How leaders apply self-determination theory in organizations. *Organization Management Journal*, 18(2), 76–94.

PAUSE AND REFLECT

How do you support autonomy, competence and relatedness in your workplace?

Impact

In my work with leaders and teams, I often return to the concept of *impact* as derived by Thomas and Velthouse[6] in their cognitive model of empowerment.

I have created Figure 3.4 to visualise the framework of the cognitive model of empowerment and understand how individuals experience empowerment at work. The four cognitive elements of meaning, competence, self-determination, and impact are not merely abstract concepts. They are the psychological levers that leaders can activate to cultivate intrinsic motivation.

Meaning, Competence, Self-Determination and Impact

Meaning Alignment between work and personal values	**Competence** Confidence in one's ability to perform tasks
Self-Determination Autonomy in initiating and regulating actions	**Impact** Belief that one's actions influence outcomes

Figure 3.4: Source: N. Bonfiglio-Pavisich, © (2025).
(Derived from: Thomas and Velthouse (1990),
Cognitive elements of empowerment.[6])

Impact refers to the degree to which individuals believe they can influence strategic, administrative, or operational outcomes. It's not about appearing busy or involved but about knowing that your contributions matter, that they have an impact. When people perceive that their actions have real consequences, they begin to see themselves as agents of change rather than passive participants. This belief fuels intrinsic motivation, deepens commitment, and fosters a sense of ownership over both tasks and outcomes. In empowered workplaces, impact is cultivated through transparent communication, meaningful delegation, and recognition of individual contributions. When employees believe that their voice shapes direction and their work drives results, they don't merely show up: they show up with purpose.

Self-determination encourages individuals to act with autonomy and initiative. Impact is experienced through autonomy and initiative, reinforcing the belief that their contributions are meaningful and valued. When these elements are present, people don't just perform, they engage, own, and thrive.

PAUSE AND REFLECT

Consider the quadrants on page 64.

- How can you as a leader lift people as you lead?
- What is the impact you have on others as they walk away from you?

As I often share with leaders I work alongside, a 2018 meta-analysis offers compelling evidence for the strategic value of empowering leadership in today's workplaces. The research, which looked at 105 independent samples, was published in the *Journal of*

Organisational Behaviour.[14] The findings demonstrate that empowering leadership significantly enhances both individual and team outcomes, including task performance, creativity, and organisational citizenship behaviours. What's particularly important is these effects hold true across diverse industries and contexts, reinforcing the idea that empowerment is not a niche strategy: it's a universal lever for performance. The meta-analysis also highlights the mechanisms through which empowerment works: trust in leadership, psychological safety, and the quality of leader–member exchange (LMX) or the relationships between leaders and followers. At the team level, collective empowerment – not individual autonomy alone – drives performance. These findings remind us that empowerment is not simply about delegation; it's about creating the conditions where people are trusted, capable, and connected. When leaders invest in these relational and psychological foundations, they don't merely boost morale – they unlock the full potential of their teams.

In my leadership development work, I draw on real-world case studies to help leaders reflect on how they can engage in leadership that lifts others. One such example is the 2024 study of Ethio-Telecom by

---

14 Lee, A., Willis, S., & Tian, A. W. (2018). Empowering leadership: A meta-analytic examination of incremental contribution, mediation, and moderation. *Journal of Organizational Behavior,* 39(3), 306–325.

Medhn Desta and Mulie.[15] They explored the impact of empowering leadership on employee performance with a particular focus on the mediating role of work engagement. After surveying 214 sales representatives in Addis Ababa with structural equation modelling, they found a clear and significant relationship: empowering leadership practices positively influenced both employee performance and engagement. Yet, the descriptive data told a different story. Empowering leadership was not widely practised, and employee engagement levels were low. Tulu, when commenting on the study, said the disconnect between leadership intention and employee experience is a critical insight for leaders: empowerment must be more than a concept; empowerment must be a lived and consistent practice.[16]

What was salient in the Ethio-Telecom study was the partial mediation effect of work engagement. In other words, empowering leadership doesn't just improve performance directly. Empowerment is facilitated through connections and a growth mindset

---

15 Medhn Desta, A. G., & Mulie, H. (2024). The effect of empowering leadership practices on employees' performance with the mediating role of work engagement: The case of Ethio-Telecom. *Cogent Business & Management*, 11(1), 2307066.

16 Tulu, D. A. (2024). Ethio-Telecom reform: An assessment from the perspective of homegrown economic reform and the imperatives of economic globalization. *Hasanuddin Journal of International Affairs*, 4(2). https://pdfs.semanticscholar.org/da9f/08b148f3426ee3164350821ca3b6740e7fbf.pdf

that serves to enhance how engaged people perceive themselves in their roles. Engagement, characterised by vigour, dedication, and absorption, emerged as a vital psychological state that amplifies the benefits of empowerment. When employees are genuinely empowered, they are more likely to bring energy, resilience, and focus to their work. Empowerment is about building trust, supporting autonomy, and creating a sense of ownership and meaning. These are the deeper layers of leadership that drive sustainable performance.

For leaders navigating complex, fast-paced environments like telecommunications, the Ethio-Telecom findings are a timely reminder: empowerment must be intentional, relational, and supported by strategies that promote engagement.[15] Delegating responsibility without cultivating psychological readiness can lead to disengagement and even burnout. Leaders must therefore create environments where people are seen, supported, and capable. They do this by offering regular feedback, recognising contributions, and providing opportunities for growth. When done well, empowerment activates the conditions that allow individuals and teams to thrive.

Cultural Considerations

I emphasise in my work with leaders across cultures and industries that empowering leadership cannot be fully effective without cultural intelligence. When workplaces establish conditions that show respect for people's cultural context in authentic ways, it empowers the workers to take ownership of their work.[17] For example, in one organisation I worked with, some women were uncomfortable with certain workplace settings because of their religious beliefs. We found alternatives that honoured everyone's dignity and expectations.

Leaders who understand the values, communication norms, and expectations of their teams are far better positioned to foster genuine empowerment. Cultural intelligence allows leaders to adapt their approach, ensuring that empowerment strategies resonate with the lived experiences of those they lead. Effective communication is a key component of cultural intelligence. Without this sensitivity, even the best intentions can be misinterpreted or fall short.

When leaders combine empowerment with cultural awareness, they create environments where people are seen, respected, and motivated

---

17 Coqual. (2020). Company spotlight: Google culture conversations in India. In *Belonging: Four Case Studies* (pp. 6–7). Coqual. https://coqual.org/wp-content/uploads/2020/12/Belonging-4-Case-Studies.pdf

to contribute. The synergy builds trust, enhances engagement, and strengthens psychological safety, especially in diverse or global teams. It's not about applying a one-size-fits-all model but about tuning into what empowerment looks and feels like for different individuals. This blend of leadership and cultural intelligence isn't merely a nice-to-have – it's a strategic necessity for unlocking the full potential of people and organisations. The urgency and importance for leaders to develop this knowledge cannot be overstated.[18]

Cultural considerations play a crucial role in how empowering leadership is perceived and practised across various regions and organisational contexts. In cultures with high power distance such as many Asian, Middle Eastern, and Latin American societies, employees may be more accustomed to hierarchical structures. These individuals may initially resist or misunderstand empowerment efforts. In these settings, empowerment must be introduced gradually and paired with clear guidance and support to avoid confusion or perceived abandonment.[19] For example, in Japan, where respect for authority and group harmony is deeply embedded, leaders who empower employees must also ensure that decisions align with collective

18 Clark, J. M., & Polesello, D. (2017). Emotional and cultural intelligence in diverse workplaces: Getting out of the box. *Industrial and Commercial Training*, 49(7/8), 337–349.

19 Alon, I., Boulanger, M., Elston, J. A., Galanaki, E., Martínez de Ibarreta, C., Meyers, J., ... & Vélez-Calle, A. (2018). Business cultural intelligence quotient: A five-country study. *Thunderbird International Business Review*, 60(3), 237–250.

values and expectations. Conversely, in low power distance cultures like the Netherlands or Australia, employees often expect autonomy and participative decision-making, which makes empowering leadership more naturally effective. Similarly, in cultures with high uncertainty avoidance such as Germany or Japan, leaders need to provide clear guidelines and structure to empower effectively. On the other hand, in cultures with low uncertainty avoidance, like the United States or the UK, leaders can empower by encouraging risk-taking and innovation

Real-world examples illustrate how cultural sensitivity enhances empowerment outcomes. At Google India, the leadership adapted empowerment strategies to fit local norms by combining autonomy with structured mentorship, ensuring that employees felt supported while taking initiative.[17] In contrast, Nordic companies like IKEA have long embraced flat hierarchies and employee autonomy, reflecting cultural values of equality and trust.[20] These examples highlight the fact that empowerment is not a one-size-fits-all approach. Empowerment must be contextualised to cultural expectations around authority, communication, and individualism. Leaders who understand and respect these cultural dynamics are better equipped to generate genuine empowerment,

---

20 Bouttell, L. (2025). What leadership style does IKEA use? A strategic analysis. *Quarterdeck*. https://quarterdeck.co.uk/articles/what-leadership-style-does-ikea-use

build trust, and drive performance across diverse teams and global organisations.

Let's consolidate our thoughts.
We began our discussion of empowerment versus enablement at work a few pages back when I noted that dynamic, evolving workplaces need to foster individual agency and collective resilience, and how achieving these outcomes involves empowerment and enablement. We looked at the four key dimensions of cognitive states that contribute to empowerment, namely meaning, competence, self-determination, and impact.

So, to be clear, empowerment and enablement each serve a different purpose. Empowering leaders are those who support autonomy by delegating decisions and encouraging initiative. Leadership that lifts others means that leaders do not merely assign tasks, they develop people. People development includes coaching, mentoring, building capacity and confidence and modelling the behaviours they wish to see. Accountability is sustained by clarifying expectations and outcomes, ensuring that individuals understand how their work contributes to broader organisational goals. Most importantly, empowering leaders builds trust by encouraging open communication and shared decision-making, creating a culture where people are safe to take ownership.

Equally important, however, is the role of enabling leadership. Before people can be empowered, they must be equipped with the knowledge, skills, and understandings required for their respective roles and aligned responsibilities. Leaders who engage in enabling practices provide the resources, tools, and systems that allow individuals to perform effectively. They provide structured guidance, feedback, and mentoring to build clarity and competence. And they create psychologically safe environments where learning, collaboration, and experimentation are not only allowed but encouraged. This is where the mantra be **present, not passive** becomes essential. Leaders must be actively engaged in supporting their teams, not simply observing from the sidelines.

Enablement is often the precursor to empowerment. Leaders must first build the foundation of skill and confidence before expecting individuals to take full ownership of their roles. This is where intentionality matters. **Be intentional, not incidental** reminds us that leadership is a deliberate act. It's about designing experiences that build their team's capability and confidence, rather than leaving development to chance. When leaders are intentional in how they enable others, they create the conditions for sustainable empowerment.

Highlighting these strategies in this chapter leads us to a practical truth: effective leadership is not about choosing between enabling and empowering. It's about sequencing them wisely. Leaders must first enable by building skills, confidence, and clarity. Only then can they empower their people by granting autonomy and encouraging ownership. Throughout this process, **be generous, not jealous** serves as a guiding principle.

Generous leaders share knowledge, opportunities, and recognition, knowing that lifting others does not diminish their own influence – it multiplies it. When this balance is struck, employees are not overwhelmed by responsibility before they are ready. Instead, they are supported, prepared, and inspired to lead from where they stand. This balanced approach is what transforms your leadership role from a solitary concentrated splash into a leadership role that creates a ripple effect that is wider, cumulative and spreads your influence across the organisation.

• • •

Takeaways

- **Meaning:** Alignment between work and personal values.

- **Competence:** Confidence in one's ability to perform.

- **Self-determination:** Autonomy in decision-making.

- **Impact:** Belief in one's ability to influence outcomes.

What will you START doing?

....

....

....

....

What will you CONTINUE doing?

....

....

....

....

What will you STOP doing?

....

....

....

....

Chapter Four

Facing the Facts: Reality Testing

Asking questions and searching for answers is a powerful tool. ~ Janine Schindler, MCC

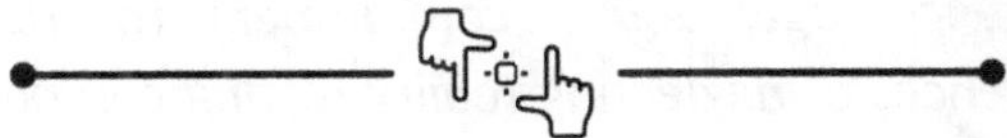

Janice stepped into her new role unaware that she was entering a team with a hidden agenda. From day one, two team members resented her presence claiming she had been "anointed, not appointed" to her position. They assigned her tasks they disliked expecting her to fail. But Janice delivered with excellence, dismantling their assumptions and proving her capability. Unable to fault her work ethic, they turned to a particular form of sabotage.

What added fuel to the fire was that Janice discovered they had created plans to connect with leaders in a way that served their own interests. The two team members created pseudonyms for their leaders – son, dad and grandpa – to secretly plot how to manipulate them into getting what they wanted. She confronted their behaviour, and the retaliation was swift: exclusion, silence, and gaslighting became her daily reality. This form of retaliation, known as 'character sabotage', involves attempts to undermine a person's reputation or credibility, often through spreading rumours or isolating the individual.

Had the leaders of these two individuals engaged in reality testing – seeking objective truth over assumption – they would have seen through their manipulation. Instead, they were used as pawns in a self-serving game. Janice's experience is a stark reminder that leadership requires vigilance, courage, and a commitment to truth. The consequences of neglecting reality testing can be severe, leading to being manipulated and used for others' gain.

What Is Reality Testing?

Reality testing is a cornerstone of emotional intelligence and offers a great many practical benefits. According to the Bar-On EQ-i 2.0 model, reality testing is the ability to see situations objectively, devoid of emotional distortion or personal bias.[1] This skill allows leaders to pause, assess, and respond to facts rather than assumptions. In high-stakes environments where clarity and composure are crucial, reality testing is essential for sound decision-making and interpersonal effectiveness. Individuals with strong reality testing can strip away emotional filters and engage with the truth of a situation, a foundational skill for effective leadership.[2]

Working with leaders who are navigating complexity and change, I recommend they return to the foundational skill of reality testing. The psychologist, Reuven Bar-On,[3] in his EQ-i model, invites us to think about reality testing as the ability to remain objective by perceiving situations as they truly are, rather than through the lens of personal bias or wishful thinking. Reality testing is a leadership imperative, not merely a cognitive skill. Leaders who practise reality testing are better equipped to make grounded decisions, especially in high-pressure environments where emotions and assumptions can easily distort

1 Stein, S. J., & Book, H. E. (2011). *The EQ edge: Emotional intelligence and your success.* John Wiley & Sons.
2 Neophytou, L. (2012). Examining the validity and reliability of the Greek version of the Bar-On's Emotional Quotient Inventory. *ResearchGate.*
3 Bar-On, R. (2004). The Bar-On Emotional Quotient Inventory (EQ-i): Rationale, description and summary of psychometric properties. In G. Geher (Ed.), *Measuring emotional intelligence: Common ground and controversy* (pp. 115–145). Nova Science Publishers. https://psycnet.apa.org/record/2004-19636-006

perception. In emotionally intelligent leadership, this capacity becomes a stabilising force, allowing leaders to respond with clarity, fairness, and focus.

Reality testing aligns closely with cognitive behavioural theory (CBT), which offers a practical framework for understanding and challenging distorted thinking patterns.

Examples of distorted thinking patterns that can cloud one's judgement include catastrophising, personalisation, or confirmation bias. I've seen this play out in leadership coaching sessions, where a leader's assumptions about a team member's intent can derail trust and collaboration. CBT encourages us to pause, reflect, and challenge these distortions. When leaders apply a CBT discipline, they improve their decision-making and model emotional regulation and psychological safety for their teams.[4]

Self-awareness has a critical role to play in reality testing. Leaders who can accurately assess their emotional responses by asking, "Is this reaction grounded in fact or filtered through my own expectations?" are better equipped to regulate their emotions and respond constructively. Such clarity not only enhances personal resilience but also strengthens empathy and communication. Leaders who model this kind of emotional discipline create a ripple effect across

---

4   Beck, J. S. (2011). *Cognitive behavior therapy: Basics and beyond* (2nd ed.). Guilford Press.

their teams, fostering cultures of trust, transparency, and psychological safety in which their team members are secure and valued.[2]

From a positive psychology perspective, reality testing is a key factor in sustaining well-being and adaptive functioning. Salovey, Mayer, and Caruso[5] have shown that emotional intelligence, when viewed as a skill, contributes to positive outcomes across relationships, education, and the workplace. Reality testing supports individuals to interpret challenges realistically and respond with clarity and optimism. It's not about denying difficulty; it's about facing it with a mindset that is both grounded and growth oriented.

A powerful insight is situated at this intersection of emotional intelligence and positive psychology. When we develop reality testing, we're doing more than improving our leadership: we're enhancing our overall capacity to flourish. It empowers us to pause, reflect, and challenge our assumptions. In doing so, we become more balanced in our reactions and more intentional in our actions. For leaders, this means creating environments where decisions are rooted in truth, not fear, and where people are empowered to act with both confidence and clarity.

---

5 Salovey, P., Mayer, J. D., & Caruso, D. (2002). The positive psychology of emotional intelligence. In C. R. Snyder & S. J. Lopez (Eds.), *Handbook of positive psychology* (pp. 159–171). Oxford University Press.

Drawing inspiration from Mayer,[6] I have created a model (Fig. 4.1) to illustrate the intersection of emotional intelligence, reality testing and positive psychology. We see how emotional intelligence serves as a foundational capability for effective leadership. Emotional intelligence encompasses four key branches: perceiving, using, understanding, and managing emotions. These competencies are the emotional architecture leaders rely on to navigate complexity and build trust.

Intersection of Emotional Intelligence & Positive Psychology

Figure 4.1: Source: N. Bonfiglio-Pavisich, © (2025).
Derived from: Mayer (2002), MSCEIT.[6])

---

6   Mayer, J. D. (2002). *MSCEIT: Mayer-Salovey-Caruso emotional intelligence test*. Toronto, Canada: Multi-Health Systems.

Reality testing plays a critical role in the intersection of emotional intelligence and positive psychology by anchoring leaders in accurate emotional perception. It's about seeing situations clearly, without distortion, and making sound decisions based on what's truly happening and not what we fear or assume.

Positive psychology and emotional intelligence strengthen reality testing by fostering optimism, resilience, and a growth mindset enabling leaders to assess situations accurately while maintaining a constructive perspective. When leaders operate from this space, they foster well-being, motivation, and meaningful connection, creating environments where people flourish, not just function.

Reality testing is a vital leadership tool that prevents impulsive decisions, groupthink, and overconfidence. It empowers leaders to challenge assumptions, seek diverse perspectives, and remain grounded in the face of pressure. By doing so, it steers leaders away from making choices based on distorted perceptions, ensuring alignment, sound strategy, and a boost in trust.

Reality testing is not about being coldly rational; it's about being clear-eyed and emotionally grounded. Leaders who cultivate this skill are more likely to be curious, not furious; be responsive and not reactive; and be doing and not stewing. You may remember these mantras from my first book, *It's All About It!*[7] When we lift others as we lead, we create environments where people are seen, heard, and empowered to contribute meaningfully.

Ultimately, reality testing is not a standalone skill: it's part of a broader emotional and psychological toolkit that supports effective, ethical, and human-centred leadership. We're cultivating wisdom (not merely improving performance) when we teach leaders to test their assumptions, challenge their thinking, and stay anchored in what is real. In our volatile geopolitical and economic environments, this wisdom, blended with the complexities of emotionally charged workplaces, is more valuable than ever. So, we need to listen rather than assume, and to lead with both confidence and humility.

Consider the following situations.

Situation One

The executive director of a nonprofit insisted on expanding programs despite declining donations and staff burnout. Ignoring financial reports and staff feedback, they argued that "passion will sustain us". Reality testing was absent, and decisions were based on optimism, not data. As a result, staff attrition soared by 40 percent within a year. The employees who

---

7 Bonfiglio-Pavisich, N. (2024). *It's all about IT!: Evidence-based, practical guide to workplace communications.* Turtle Publishing.

remained faced overwhelming workloads, reducing productivity. Donor confidence eroded due to visible instability. Ultimately, leadership credibility collapsed, and the organisation downsized drastically.

Situation Two

A principal launched a new digital curriculum without assessing teacher readiness or infrastructure. They dismissed concerns and assumed that "teachers will adapt quickly".

No pilot testing or stakeholder consultation occurred. Teachers felt unsupported, leading to frustration and mid-year resignations. Student outcomes declined as educators struggled with unfamiliar tools. Morale plummeted and trust in leadership eroded. The school faced reputational damage and found it difficult to attract quality staff.

Situation Three

A CEO who mandated a return-to-office policy ignored employee surveys favouring hybrid work and market trends, arguing that "physical presence equals productivity". Reality testing was absent and there was no analysis of attrition risk or competitor practices. When top talent left for flexible employers, turnover costs increased. The remaining staff were disengaged, which in turn reduced overall productivity. Innovation slowed as collaboration suffered under rigid structures. Shareholder confidence dipped, bringing into question the leader's adaptability.

PAUSE AND REFLECT

- What gets in the way of a leader's capacity to test reality?

- How does reality testing apply to you?

- How do you check your assumptions?

My leadership coaching and development work often draws on the insights of Daniel Kahneman's dual-system theory to deepen leaders' understanding of reality testing. In his seminal work, *Thinking, Fast and Slow*, Kahneman[8] introduces two modes of thinking. System 1 is fast, intuitive, and emotionally driven. System 2 is slower, more deliberate, and analytical. Although System 1 serves us well in routine decisions, it is where bias and error tend to reside. Reality testing, as a leadership skill, requires us to consciously engage System 2 to slow down, question our assumptions, and examine the facts before drawing conclusions. This is especially critical in high-stakes environments where reactive thinking can lead to costly misjudgements.

---

8 Kahneman, D. (2011). *Thinking, fast and slow*. Farrar, Straus and Giroux.

In practice, I've seen how reality testing transforms leadership behaviour. Consider a classic System 1 response: a leader instinctively assumes a team member is disengaged due to laziness. A System 2 leader who is grounded in reality testing would pause, examine the data, consider the broader context, and perhaps initiate a conversation to understand the whole picture. This shift from reactive to reflective thinking not only improves decision-making but also strengthens relationships and trust within teams. It's a move from assumption to inquiry, from judgement to curiosity. Another example is a leader who is considering a new business strategy. Instead of immediately dismissing it as too risky, they engage in reality testing by gathering data, seeking diverse perspectives, and challenging their own biases before making a decision.

What I find particularly powerful is how this approach supports a more inclusive and emotionally intelligent leadership style. Leaders who engage in reality testing are more likely to listen deeply, challenge their own narratives, and create space for diverse perspectives. It leads to better outcomes but enables psychological safety and a culture of fairness while doing so. Reality testing plays a crucial role in fostering a culture in which everyone's voice is heard, and decisions are based on facts and diverse perspectives. In today's complex and emotionally charged workplaces, that kind of leadership is not optional – it's essential.

Ultimately, reality testing is more than a cognitive function because it requires disciplined leadership. It calls us to be intentional, to resist the pull of fast thinking, and to lead with clarity and compassion. When leaders develop this skill, they make better decisions as well as model the kind of thoughtful, grounded presence that inspires trust and drives sustainable performance.

Reality testing requires leaders to pause and reflect, engaging the System 2 mode to challenge cognitive biases and emotional reactions that may distort perception. It is especially important in high-stakes or ambiguous situations. For instance, during a crisis, a leader in System 1 mode might make reactive decisions based on fear or urgency, such as cutting resources or blaming individuals. However, a leader who activates the System 2 mode has a more measured response after gathering data, consulting stakeholders, and considering long-term implications. Reality testing is crucial in preventing impulsive decisions and ensuring a more measured, thoughtful approach.

In practice, leaders who fail to balance these two systems may fall into decision traps. Consider the 2008 financial crisis: many executives relied on intuitive judgements and market momentum (System 1), ignoring warning signs and failing to test the reality of unsustainable practices. In contrast, leaders who engaged System 2 thinking, such as those who pulled out of risky investments early, demonstrated vigorous reality testing. Kahneman's theory emphasises that –

although intuition has its place – deliberate, reflective thinking will ensure decisions are grounded in reality, not assumptions. Developing this skill benefits leaders to lead with clarity, reduce risk, and build trust through thoughtful, evidence-based actions.

Let's examine a formula that I use with my clients to engage effectively in reality testing. In Figure 4.2 the formula is R = D + E + V. Reality (R) equals data (D) plus external perspectives (E) plus verification (V).

The Reality Testing Formula

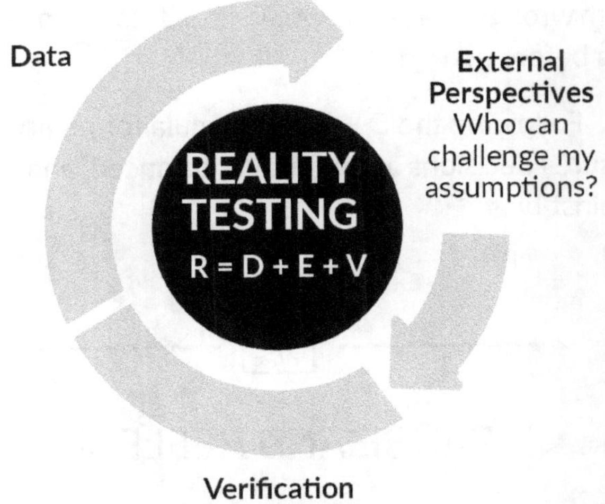

Figure 4.2: Source: N. Bonfiglio-Pavisich, © (2025).

Effective reality testing begins with gathering data or measurable facts to ground decisions in evidence rather than assumptions.

Step One: Data – Gather measurable facts:
What evidence supports this decision? What trends or metrics confirm it?

Step Two: External Perspectives – Seek input:
Who can challenge my thinking and assumptions and provide diverse viewpoints? What do stakeholders think? Who can help identify blind spots?

Step Three: Verification – Stress-test assumptions:
If I'm wrong, what signs would I see? How can I validate this before acting?

Following the D + E + V formula for reality testing ensures decisions are informed, balanced, and resilient against bias.

PAUSE AND REFLECT

Think about a current workplace situation. Apply the R = D + E + V formula.

- Where is the gap between effective reality testing and failed reality testing?

Why Reality Testing Matters for Leaders

Leaders are constantly faced with decisions that affect people, strategy, and culture. Reality testing ensures that these decisions are grounded in evidence, not assumptions or emotional reactions. For example, a leader who assumes a team is disengaged based on a few vocal complaints may overlook broader data showing high morale and productivity. Without reality testing, this leader might implement unnecessary changes and disrupt a well-functioning team.

Moreover, reality testing helps leaders navigate ambiguity and complexity. In times of crisis or rapid change, leaders must distinguish between what is known, what is unknown, and what is speculation. Such clarity enables better risk management, communication, and strategic planning. Leaders who practise reality testing are also more likely to encourage psychological safety, a concept that refers to an environment where team members are safe to take risks and be vulnerable in front of one another. Leaders who model openness to feedback and a willingness to question their own assumptions contribute to this psychological safety.

Real-World Examples: When Reality Testing Fails

Case 1: Kodak's Missed Opportunity

Kodak famously failed to adapt to the digital photography revolution, despite having developed the first digital camera in 1975. Leadership dismissed the threat of digital technology, believing film would remain dominant. In the absence of reality testing, market trends and consumer behaviour were ignored, leading to the company's decline. Had leaders objectively assessed the data and challenged their assumptions, Kodak might have led the digital transformation instead of being left behind.[9]

Case 2: Uber's Culture Crisis

Under former CEO Travis Kalanick, Uber faced numerous scandals related to workplace culture, ethics, and leadership behaviour. Reports of toxic culture were dismissed or minimised, and leadership failed to test the reality of employee experiences. It led to reputational damage, legal challenges, and a leadership overhaul. Because there was no reality testing, internal signals were ignored, and external feedback created

---

9 Osum. (2024). *A deep dive into the Kodak case study*. Osum. https://www.osum.com/deep-dive-into-kodak-case-study

a disconnect between leadership perception and organisational reality.[10]

Reality testing is more than a cognitive skill: it's a leadership imperative. In a world of rapid change, complex systems, and diverse teams, leaders must be able to discern truth from perception and act with clarity. Those who master reality testing are better equipped to lead with integrity, make sound decisions, and build trust. They create cultures where truth is valued, feedback is welcomed, and strategy is grounded in reality.

I maintain that leaders must **be present, not passive**; and actively engage with facts, listen deeply, and observe signals rather than ignore them. They should **be generous, not jealous**, by inviting diverse perspectives and valuing input instead of guarding authority or resisting challenge. Finally, they must **be intentional, not incidental**, by approaching decisions with purpose and rigour rather than reacting impulsively or relying on assumptions.

When leaders apply reality testing, the ability to remain objective and accurately assess situations means they can better lift others as they lead. This skill helps distinguish between assumptions and facts,

---

10 Burns, U. (2025, July 4). Uber's leadership crisis: Transforming from toxic culture to ethical governance. CEO Today. https://www.ceotodaymagazine.com/2025/07/ubers-leadership-crisis-transforming-from-toxic-culture-to-ethical-governance/

especially in emotionally charged or complex workplace scenarios. By staying grounded and encouraging others to do the same, leaders foster clarity and fairness. For example, when an employee feels overlooked for a promotion, a leader using reality testing might guide the conversation towards specific performance metrics and development goals, rather than allowing the discussion to spiral into blame or resentment.

Conversely, when reality testing is absent, a leader's reaction might be based on bias, emotion, or incomplete information, which can escalate conflict and erode trust. Employees may perceive they are misunderstood or unfairly judged, particularly when decisions are made without considering all relevant perspectives. In such cases, the leader's inability to test reality objectively can damage morale and hinder team cohesion.

Ultimately, reality testing allows leaders to lead with clarity, compassion, and credibility. By modelling this skill and living the mantras of being present, generous, and intentional, leaders not only improve decision-making but also elevate the emotional intelligence of their teams, creating workplaces where challenges are met with insight and collaboration rather than confusion or defensiveness.

• • •

Takeaways

- Decisions need evidence, not assumptions.

- Seek diverse perspectives to avoid blind spots.

- Validate before acting.

- Ignoring reality signals has consequences.

- Challenge the perspectives of others.

What will you START doing?

What will you CONTINUE doing?

What will you STOP doing?

Chapter Five

Knowing Through Experience: A Dual Force for Leadership

Information is not knowledge. The only source of knowledge is experience. ~ Albert Einstein

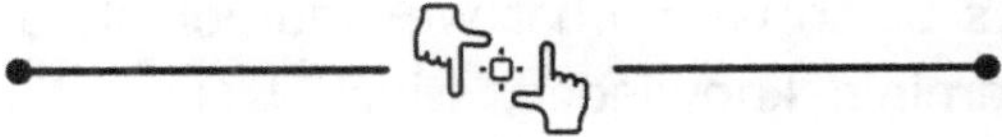

In a high-stakes project meeting, a newly appointed manager presents a data-driven strategy to streamline operations. Her proposal is backed by the latest research, industry benchmarks, and predictive analytics. Sitting across from her is a veteran team leader who's seen three restructures and knows the terrain intimately. He listens, nods, and then gently points out a cultural nuance in the team that could derail the plan if not addressed. Together, they revise the strategy; her knowledge shapes the vision,

his experience grounds it in reality. The result? A plan that is both innovative and executable. This is the power of knowledge and experience working in tandem.

As someone who has spent years observing and mentoring leaders across sectors, I've often reflected on the delicate interplay between what we know and what we've lived. Leadership is rarely about choosing between knowledge and experience but more about understanding how they complement one another. Although formal learning equips us with frameworks and tools, lived experience provides the context and judgement to apply them wisely. This distinction is empowering. When we understand the unique contributions of both, we can lead with greater clarity, agility, and impact, feeling confident and capable.[1]

Let's begin with what we traditionally associate with learning: knowledge, which is the structured, often formal, accumulation of information. The accumulation of information is what we gain through study, training, and exposure to new ideas. It's the foundation upon which many careers are built. Individuals who work primarily with information, often referred to as knowledge workers, are those who use

---

1   Maor, D., Hans-Werner, K., Strovink, K., & Srinivasan, R. (2024, August 19). *The versatile leader: How learning to adapt makes CEOs better.* McKinsey & Company.

their expertise to drive innovation and transformation across industries.[2] They are the ones who bring new ideas and concepts to the table, shaping the future of their organisations and industries. However, knowledge can sometimes be too abstract. It may lack the nuance required to navigate complex, real-world challenges, especially when divorced from context or practical application.[3]

The knowledge gap trap in decision-making occurs when leaders rely heavily on theoretical or codified knowledge without integrating the lived, contextual insights that come from experience. Such imbalance can lead to decisions that read well on paper but falter in practice. For instance, a manager might implement a new workflow based on industry best practices without consulting frontline staff who understand the nuances of daily operations. The result? Resistance, inefficiency, and missed opportunities for adaptation.[4]

On the other hand, experience brings a different kind of wisdom. Experience is shaped by trial and

---

2   Alavi, M., & Westerman, G. (2023, November 7). How generative AI will transform knowledge work. *Harvard Business Review.* https://hbr.org/2023/11/how-generative-ai-will-transform-knowledge-work

3   Atir, S., & Dunning, D. (2024, September). Research: Competent leaders know the limits of their expertise. *Harvard Business Review.*

4   Jones, B. F. (2008). The knowledge trap: Human capital and development reconsidered (NBER Working Paper No. 14138). National Bureau of Economic Research. https://www.nber.org/papers/w14138

error and the passage of time. It teaches us not only what works, but why it works, and when it doesn't. I recall a case shared by Janson[5] where a future CFO was intentionally rotated through diverse roles across countries to build the breadth of insight needed for a CFO role. This kind of experiential learning strengthens intuition, emotional intelligence, and pattern recognition, qualities that are difficult to teach but essential for effective leadership. Similarly, research by Anselmann and Mulder[6] reinforces this, finding that individuals with high experiential insight are better equipped to anticipate challenges and adapt strategies in dynamic environments.

The Pros and Cons: A Balanced View

In my experience, knowledge offers breadth and insights. It opens doors to new possibilities and assists us to stay current in a rapidly changing world. Knowledge can be used to determine the gap in the capacity and agency of individuals.[5] Experience, on the other hand, offers depth. It provides insight into human behaviour, organisational culture, and the subtleties of

---

5　Janson, K. (2021, June 7). The paradox of judgement and experience: How to develop a leaders' ability to make good decisions. *Forbes Coaches Council.*

6　Anselmann, V., & Mulder, R. H. (2020). Transformational leadership, knowledge sharing and reflection, and work teams' performance: A structural equation modelling analysis. *Journal of Nursing Management,* 28(7), 1627–1634.

timing. Benkert and van Dam[7] explain how experiential learning involves acquiring experience by asking key questions:

- What needs doing? (Consider the experience and the exploration)

- What needs to happen? (Consider sharing and reflecting)

- What is essential? (Consider processing and analysing)

- Why is it important? (Consider understanding the context and conditions)

- How can it work for me? (Consider the application)

The Taoist philosophy that underpins Landsberg's[8] coaching model encourages leaders to act in harmony with the natural flow of human behaviour and workplace dynamics. Taoism values balance, non-coercion, and effortless action, the principles that align closely with the idea of nurturing both skill and will without force.

The Skill/Will model (Figure 5.1) categorises individuals based on two dimensions: skill (their capability and experience) and will (their motivation

---

7   Benkert, C., & van Dam, N. (2015, August 1). *Experiential learning: What's missing in most change programs.* McKinsey & Company.

8   Landsberg, M. (2015). *The Tao of Coaching: Boost your effectiveness at work by inspiring and developing those around you* (Updated ed.). Profile Books. ISBN 9781781253328.

and engagement).[9] The matrix includes four quadrants: Low Skill/High Will individuals who are eager novices, High Skill/Low Will people who are stereotypically grumpy experts, High Skill/High Will performers, best described as shining stars, and Low Skill/Low Will people who tend to be doubtful performers. This model emphasises the need for leadership to recognise that an individual with a unique combination of skill and will needs a tailored approach such as coaching, motivating, delegating, or guiding, to support them to grow and contribute effectively.

The Skill/Will Matrix

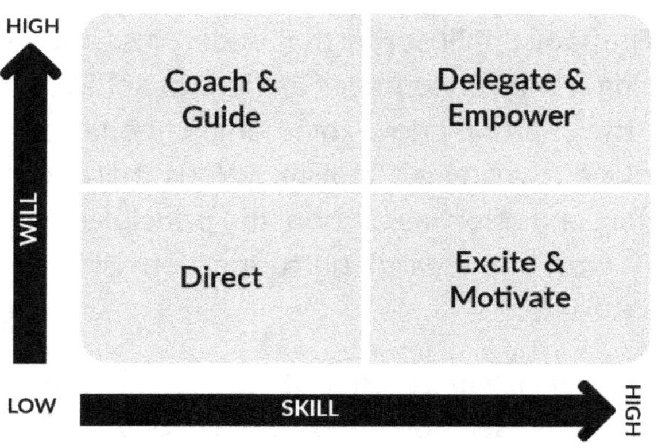

Figure 5.1:Adapted: Gardner (2024), A complete guide to the Skill Will Matrix.[9]

---

9   Gardner, R. (2024). *A complete guide to the Skill Will Matrix.* AIHR. https://www.aihr.com/blog/skill-will-matrix

For example, a *High Will / Low Skill* employee benefits from structured coaching and encouragement, whereas a High Skill / Low Will employee who is not motivated might need inspiration or a new challenge to excite, motivate and reignite their engagement.

High-performing *High Skill / High Will* team members bring both capability and drive. They consistently deliver strong results and often seek out new challenges. These individuals thrive when trusted with autonomy and meaningful responsibilities. However, without recognition or opportunities for growth, they may become disengaged. To keep them motivated, leaders should delegate strategically, offer stretch assignments, and ensure their contributions are acknowledged.

In contrast, enthusiastic but inexperienced *Low Skill / High Will* employees bring energy and a willingness to learn, even if they lack the technical skills to excel independently. Their motivation makes them ideal candidates for structured development. With the right support, such as training, mentoring, and clear guidance individuals can quickly grow into valuable contributors. When we lift others to lead, we should focus on building the employee's confidence while gradually increasing their responsibilities.

Then there are skilled individuals who appear disengaged (*High Skill / Low Will*). Though they possess the expertise, their motivation may be lacking due to burnout, boredom, or misalignment with their goals. These employees require a different approach: uncovering the root of their disengagement, reigniting their interest, and offering them autonomy in areas that align with their strengths. When re-engaged, they can become powerful assets to the team.

Finally, *Low Skill / Low Will* employees who struggle with both skill and motivation need clear direction and consistent support. Their underperformance may stem from unclear expectations, poor role fit, or personal challenges. Rather than writing them off, leaders should focus on setting clear goals, provide regular feedback, and create a supportive environment that encourages growth. With time and effort, even these team members can improve and contribute meaningfully.

Applying the Skill / Will Matrix in leadership enables leaders to make more informed and compassionate decisions. It encourages leaders to observe, reflect, and respond rather than react impulsively. For instance, instead of reprimanding a low-performing employee, a leader would seek to understand the root cause, whether it's a lack of skill, motivation, or a mismatch with the role. Similarly, high-performing employees should not be left unattended because they require ongoing challenges and recognition to maintain their momentum. This approach both improves individual performance and enhances team cohesion and organisational culture. By aligning leadership strategies with the natural tendencies of employees, organisations can cultivate a workplace that thrives on mutual respect, continuous development, and authentic engagement.

Bridging the Gap: Evidence-Based Integration

The most effective leaders are those who bridge the gap between knowledge and experience. A meta-analysis conducted by Bonini and colleagues[10] found that leaders who combined formal education with diverse work experiences were more adaptable, resilient, and capable of leading through uncertainty. These leaders don't only know what the textbook says; they understand how to apply it in messy, unpredictable environments. They show up with both the tools and the wisdom to lead. Such integration is not accidental; it's cultivated through reflection, mentorship, and a commitment to lifelong learning. An emphasis on continuous learning should inspire leaders to keep growing and evolving.

Gautam Mukunda[11] examined individuals in top roles across various sectors. He sorted them into two

---

10 Bonini, A., Panari, C., Caricati, L., & Mariani, M. G. (2024). The relationship between leadership and adaptive performance: A systematic review and meta-analysis. *PLOS ONE*, 19(10), e0304720. https://doi.org/10.1371/journal.pone.0304720
11 Mukunda, G. (2012). *Indispensable: When leaders really matter.* Harvard Business Review Press.

types: those who advanced through conventional paths and those who arrived through unusual or unexpected routes. He evaluated how each group performed using historical assessments in the case of US presidents. His findings revealed that those who came through unconventional means tended to have more extreme outcomes, either excelling or underperforming, while those who followed more traditional paths generally achieved moderate results. Food for thought?

Yet, experience is not without its limitations. I've observed that experiences can be shaped by outdated assumptions or environments that no longer reflect current realities which is why innovation can sometimes be hindered if relying solely on past practice. The key is for leaders to blend knowledge and experience to be better positioned to make informed, adaptive decisions. By drawing on theory while remaining grounded in practice, they can innovate without losing sight of what has worked before.

Cultivating Both: A Leadership Imperative

To lead well, we must cultivate both knowledge and experience by encouraging continuous learning through courses, reading, and dialogue, while also valuing the lessons embedded in our daily work. It means creating environments where younger employees can learn from seasoned mentors and where experienced professionals remain open to new ideas. Organisations that foster this dual development are more innovative, inclusive, and resilient. They don't just survive change: they lead it.

Consider the navigation through the knowledge and experience gap as shown in Figure 5.2.

Navigating the Knowledge and Experience Gap

Old Knowledge Lots of experience	**New Knowledge** Lots of experience
Limited Knowledge Limited experience	**New Knowledge** No experience

Figure 5.2: Source: N. Bonfiglio-Pavisich, © (2025).

Quadrant 1 Old knowledge, lots of experience
Individuals located in this quadrant rely heavily on established practices and have deep experience in their field.

- **Strengths:** High confidence, efficiency, and mastery of traditional methods.

- **Risks:** May resist innovation, overlook new trends, or rely on outdated assumptions that no longer apply.

Quadrant 2 New knowledge, lots of experience

The individuals who meet the quadrant 2 requirements combine deep experience with current, updated knowledge.

- **Strengths:** They are adaptable, insightful, and capable of applying new ideas with seasoned judgement. This combination of strengths is ideal for leadership, mentoring, and driving change while maintaining stability.

- **Risks:** Sometimes decisions can be made based on misjudgements or errors, especially if the new knowledge challenges or contradicts established practices.

Quadrant 3 Limited Knowledge, limited experience

This quadrant draws individuals who are beginners or new entrants with minimal exposure and learning.

- **Strengths:** With the right development, they can grow into any of the other quadrants.

- **Risks:** Require close guidance, training, and support to build both competence and confidence.

Quadrant 4 New Knowledge, no experience

Individuals who meet the criteria of quadrant 4 have learned new concepts but haven't yet applied them practically.

- **Strengths:** Fresh perspectives, enthusiasm, and openness to experimentation.

- **Risks:** May misapply knowledge or struggle with real-world complexities without experiential grounding.

PAUSE AND REFLECT

- Where do you fit into the knowledge and experience gap?

- Consider the team you lead or of which you are a part. Where do you believe each of the team members belong in the knowledge and experience gap trap?

The knowledge and experience gap trap exists when leaders rely heavily on theoretical or codified knowledge without integrating the lived, contextual insights that come from experience, or vice versa.

Consider some real-world applications.

Healthcare

A newly-graduated nurse may know the textbook procedures for patient care (knowledge), but handling a patient in distress requires calmness, empathy, and quick decision-making developed through experience. Is this about knowledge or experience?

Data analyst in a traditional marketing team

An experienced marketer may rely on gut instinct and past campaigns, whereas a data analyst uses real-time analytics to uncover trends and optimise strategies, often outperforming intuition. Is this about knowledge or experience?

Engineering

An engineer might understand the principles of structural design, but only through experience can they anticipate real-world challenges like material fatigue or environmental stress. Is this about knowledge and or experience?

Cybersecurity

Veteran IT staff may overlook emerging threats due to outdated practices, whereas a cybersecurity expert applies current threat intelligence and protocols to prevent breaches more effectively. Is this about knowledge and or experience?

PAUSE AND REFLECT

Consider Table 5.1. What does the knowledge and experience gap look, and sound like in your workplace?

Knowledge vs. Experience: A Comparative View

Aspect	Knowledge	Experience
Source	Education, training, research	Practice, Observation, Interaction
Transferability	Easily shared	Harder to transfer
Reliability	Consistent across contexts	Context-dependent
Development	Through study	Through doing
Value in Crisis	Offers frameworks and options	Offers intuition and judgement

Table 5.1: Source: N. Bonfiglio-Pavisich, © (2025).

When leaders possess the capacity to lift others through empathy, clarity, and empowerment, they are better equipped to address challenges among employees who are caught in the knowledge and experience trap. The gap occurs when individuals either have strong theoretical knowledge but lack practical experience, or vice versa. Leaders with strong interpersonal and communication skills can recognise these imbalances and respond with tailored support (Refer to Table 5.1). For example, they might pair a knowledgeable but inexperienced employee with a seasoned mentor, creating a learning partnership that benefits both parties.

It's worthwhile considering for a moment a Harvard Business impact study[12] that surveyed more than eleven hundred leaders in learning and development as well as human resources across fourteen countries. The study highlights a clear shift towards AI fluency, strategic adaptability, and scalable learning. These findings underscore the growing gap between traditional leadership experience and the new knowledge required to lead in digitally transforming environments. Leaders today must not only embrace emerging technologies but also learn to guide their teams through complex, tech-driven change. Outcome-focused training is now essential, aligning leadership capabilities with

---

12 Harvard Business Impact. (2025). *2025 Global Leadership Development Study: Fast, fluid, and future-focused learning.* Harvard Business Publishing. https://www.harvardbusiness. org/insight/2025-global-leadership-development-study/

innovation, agility, and future-readiness. In this new environment, we must move beyond relying on what has worked in the past and instead cultivate a mindset of continuous learning and curiosity. Bridging the gap between knowledge and experience requires humility, openness, and a commitment to growth.

When leaders do not have the capacity to bridge the gap between knowledge and experience, the knowledge–experience gap can lead to frustration, miscommunication, and underperformance. Employees may perceive they are undervalued or misunderstood, especially if their strengths are overlooked or their weaknesses are criticised without guidance. A leader who cannot lift others may default to judgement or rigid expectations, which can deepen the divide and erode morale. In such environments, talented individuals may disengage or leave, and collaboration suffers due to a lack of trust and psychological safety.

It goes without saying that we must be vigilant about how our own experience can unintentionally create bias and marginalise the voices around us. Du et al[13] reveal that, when leadership decisions are driven primarily by personal experience, they can suppress knowledge sharing and stifle innovation. This highlights a critical gap in which experience, though

---

13 Du, S., Xie, W., & Wang, J. (2022). How leaders' bias tendency affects employees' knowledge hiding behavior: The mediating role of workplace marginalization perception. *Frontiers in Psychology*, 13, 965972.

valuable, may hinder the flow of new knowledge within teams. To close this gap, leaders need to initiate emotional commitment and psychological safety, encouraging open dialogue and diverse perspectives. True leadership today requires both wisdom from the past as well as a conscious effort to remain curious about the present and to be inclusive and knowledge driven.

Conversely, when leaders actively lift others as they lead, they create a culture where learning and growth are normalised. They communicate that both knowledge and experience are valuable and that the gaps are opportunities, not flaws. These leaders use feedback loops, coaching conversations, and inclusive dialogue to enable employees to reflect, learn, and stretch beyond their current capabilities. For instance, a leader might say, "You've got a solid grasp of the theory, let's find a project where you can apply it and build confidence". This kind of support transforms the trap into a stepping stone.

Ultimately, leadership practices that lift others foster adaptive and resilient teams. They help individuals move from being stuck to feeling supported, and from uncertainty to capability. By recognising and addressing the knowledge–experience gap with compassion and strategic communication, leaders resolve immediate challenges and also build a stronger and more capable workforce. Taking this approach aligns with modern leadership principles to prioritise development, inclusion, and shared success.

PAUSE AND REFLECT

Consider the following questions:

Personal Reflection

- What assumptions do I make about people who are *book smart* versus those who are *street smart*?

- Have I ever dismissed someone's input because they lacked a qualification or title? What did I miss?

Team Dynamics

- How do I respond when someone with less experience challenges my viewpoint?

- Do I create space for both emerging knowledge and seasoned experience in team discussions?

- Are there voices in my team that go unheard because their experience isn't formalised?

Organisational Culture

- Does our workplace culture favour innovation (knowledge) or tradition (experience)? How does that show up?

- Are we more likely to promote people based on credentials or demonstrated wisdom? What does that say about us?

Leadership Practice

- How do I balance data-driven decisions with gut instinct?

- What biases do I hold about age, tenure, or education when assessing someone's capability to lead?

- Am I open to learning from those with less experience than me? What might they see that I don't?

We can overcome the knowledge–experience gap and the will and skill divide

To help people understand the value of gaining new knowledge and experiences in the workplace, leaders should adopt a three-dimensional proactive and intentional approach. First, they need to create a culture that values learning. This means openly celebrating curiosity, innovation, and growth. Leaders can model this behaviour by sharing what they're learning, encouraging questions, and showing that mistakes are part of the learning process. When employees see that acquiring new knowledge is not only accepted but expected, they're more likely to embrace it themselves. Leaders should also connect learning to purpose, explaining how new knowledge contributes to individual goals, team success, and the broader mission of the organisation.[5]

Second, leaders must provide opportunities and remove barriers to learning and experience. This includes offering access to training programs, workshops, mentorship, and collaborative or cross-functional projects. It also means giving employees the time and space to explore new ideas without fear of failure. Leaders should identify and support stretch assignments involving tasks that challenge employees to grow beyond their current skill set. By doing so, they support team members to build confidence and competence simultaneously. Importantly, leaders should tailor these opportunities to individual needs, recognising that people learn in different ways and at different paces.[10]

The third dimension is when leaders communicate the tangible benefits of new knowledge and experience. This involves showing how learning leads to better performance, career advancement, and increased job satisfaction. Leaders can use real-life examples to illustrate the impact, such as employees who took on new challenges and achieved success. They should also link learning to adaptability, especially in industries that are rapidly evolving. When employees understand that staying current and gaining diverse experiences makes them more resilient and valuable, they're more likely to invest in their own development. By reinforcing this message consistently, leaders can shift mindsets and build a workforce that thrives on continuous improvement.[6]

Knowledge and experience are not opposing forces but complementary assets. Knowledge provides the foundation, while experience adds depth and adaptability. In a rapidly changing work environment, the synergy between the two enables individuals and organisations to innovate, solve problems, and thrive. The ideal employee blends knowledge and experience, but organisations benefit from both profiles. Knowledge-rich employees bring innovation and analytical rigour, while experience-rich employees provide practical insight and stability. The key is to nurture collaboration, continuous learning, and mutual respect between the two assets.

To truly bridge the gap between knowledge and experience, leaders must embrace a mindset that is both reflective and forward-looking. Experience offers depth but, without fresh knowledge, it can be a trap that limits growth and innovation. That's why leaders must **be present, not passive**: actively engaging with new ideas rather than relying solely on what they've always known. They must **be generous, not jealous**: creating space for others to contribute knowledge and challenge assumptions. And above all, they must **be intentional, not incidental**: shaping their leadership through conscious learning and purposeful action rather than habit or tradition.

• • •

Takeaways

- Knowledge is dynamic, not static.

- Experience shapes perspective.

- Tacit knowledge is often undervalued.

- Knowledge sharing builds resilience.

- Experience doesn't equal expertise.

What will you START doing?

What will you CONTINUE doing?

What will you STOP doing?

Chapter Six

Speak to Connect

The art of communication is the language of leadership. ~ James Humes

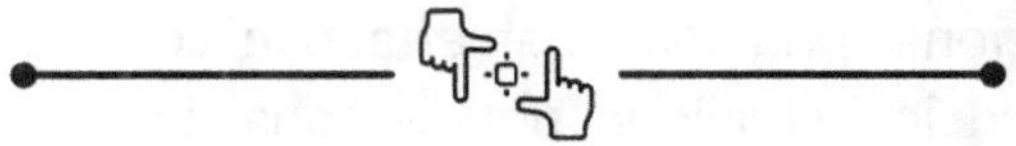

Jordan was a highly skilled strategist known for her creativity, dedication, and ability to bring teams together. She had consistently delivered results and was often the quiet force behind major project successes. Yet her manager, Alex, rarely offered her clear direction or feedback. Meetings were vague, expectations shifted without explanation and, when Jordan sought clarity, she was met with dismissiveness. Compassion was absent. Alex never asked how she was managing her workload or acknowledged the pressures she was under. Instead, communication seemed transactional and cold, leaving Jordan isolated and undervalued.

Over time, Alex's lack of authenticity and vulnerability created a barrier between them. Jordan, feeling unsafe to share her ideas or challenges, saw her contributions go unnoticed. Despite her significant impact, there were neither words of affirmation, nor celebration of her achievements. This eventually led to Jordan's departure. Her exit, though quiet, had a resounding effect. Jordan's absence left a void in both morale and performance. Alex was unaware of the reasons behind her departure, and the team lost not just a talented employee but a leader in her own right.

In my previous book, *It's All About It!*,[1] I explored the foundational principle that effective communication is rooted in behaviour, not personal judgement. By focusing on observable actions, what I termed *It!* rather than assumptions about personality, we can foster more transparent, more respectful, and accountable interactions in the workplace. This approach reduces defensiveness and opens the door to constructive conversations, even in challenging situations.

When we speak to connect, we celebrate the art of communication. While the principles of *It!* remain vital, speaking to connect is a leadership imperative. *The What? So What? Now What?* framework offers a

---

1 Bonfiglio-Pavisich, N. (2024). *It's all about IT!: Evidence-based, practical guide to workplace communications.* Turtle Publishing.

modern, structured approach to meaningful dialogue, helping leaders move from facts to relevance to action. This framework encourages leaders to go beyond information delivery and instead promote understanding and alignment. When we speak to connect, we create space for others to be seen, heard, and valued, which is where trust begins. As leaders, our words shape culture, and our conversations shape relationships.[2]

A relational approach to leadership, as described by Jim Ferrell in *You and We*[3] reframes communication as a shared experience rather than a solo performance. Connection doesn't happen in our heads; it occurs in the space between us. Ferrell's work reminds us that the real power of leadership lies not in managing individuals, but in nurturing the relationships between them. That insight aligns with fifty years of leadership communication research, which shows that leaders who communicate with authenticity, empathy, and strategic intent are more likely to inspire trust, engagement, and performance. Speaking to connect is more than a technique; it's a mindset. It's about being present, listening deeply, and leading with humanity.

---

2   Liu, E. H., Chambers, C. R., & Moore, C. (2023). Fifty years of research on leader communication: What we know and where we are going. *The Leadership Quarterly*, 34(6), 1–19. https://doi.org/10.1016/j.leaqua.2023.101734
3   Ferrell, J. (2024). *You and We: A relational rethinking of work, life, and leadership*. Matt Holt Books.

To foster increased connection, our communication must include:

- **Clarity with Compassion** – how leaders can communicate with precision while remaining empathetic.

- **Authenticity and Vulnerability** – the power of being honest and open to build trust.

- **Affirmation and Recognition** – the importance of acknowledging others to inspire and motivate.

- **Visionary Storytelling** – using narrative to connect people to purpose and possibility.

Foster Increased Connection

Clarity &
Compassion

Authenticity
& Vulnerability

Affirmation
& Recognition

Visionary
Storytelling

These elements are not simply techniques; they are transformative tools that will guide leaders to create environments where people are seen, heard, and empowered. Consider them. How might you use them in your workplace to lift others as you lead?

Clarity with Compassion

I often speak to leaders and educators about the power of clarity with compassion. These two qualities are not opposites; rather, they are partners in effective leadership. Clarity is about being direct, consistent, and transparent. It's how we communicate expectations, goals, and feedback in ways that empower others to act with confidence.[4] But clarity alone isn't enough. Compassion is what makes clarity human. It's the ability to notice, empathise, and respond to the emotional realities of those we lead. Compassionate leadership is authentically strategic; it is not soft. It builds trust, develops resilience, and creates the psychological safety that teams need to thrive.[5]

I've begun drawing on the findings of *The Love Leadership Study* initiated by Margot Faraci.[6] The study revealed a troubling trend: one in three emerging leaders is motivated primarily by fear, contributing to billions in economic losses across Australia, the US and the UK. Fear-based leadership manifests in anxiety, imposter syndrome, and disengagement, all of which erode connection and communication. The call to action

---

4   Bodell, L. (2025, August 27). The call for clarity: Why we must redefine leadership now. *Forbes Women Publication.* https://www.forbes.com/sites/lisabodell/2025/08/27/the-call-for-clarity-why-we-must-redefine-leadership-now/

5   Sinek, S. (2017). *Leaders eat last: Why some teams pull together and others don't.* Portfolio Penguin

6   Faraci, M. (2023). Love *Leadership Survey. First and First Consulting.* https://www.margotfaraci.com/loveleadershipsurvey

is clear. We need a shift towards love-based leadership, where clarity, compassion, and courage replace fear. This imperative is supported in research by Pansini and colleagues[7] which found that compassionate leadership significantly enhances employee well-being and indirectly boosts engagement. Compassionate leaders create emotionally supportive environments that foster collaboration, trust, and sustainable performance. Leadership is less about what we say and more about how we make people feel when we say it.

Authenticity and Vulnerability

Authentic leadership impacts employee resilience and performance.[8] Authentic leaders demonstrate self-awareness, relational transparency, and strong moral values. They create environments where people are seen, heard, and valued. Authenticity boosts creativity, job satisfaction, and organisational commitment. In times of uncertainty, this kind of leadership is even

---

7 Pansini, M., Buonomo, I., & Benevene, P. (2024). Fostering sustainable workplace through leaders' compassionate behaviors: Understanding the role of employee well-being and work engagement. *Sustainability, 16*(23), 10697. https://doi.org/10.3390/su162310697

8 Srimongkolkul, P., & Boriraj, J. (2024). Effects of authentic leadership on employee work performance, moderated by employee resilience. In S. Kot, B. Khalid, & A. u. Haque (Eds.), *Corporate practices: Policies, methodologies, and insights in organizational management* (pp. xx–xx). Springer. https://doi.org/10.1007/978-981-97-0996-0_42

more critical. When employees perceive their leaders as genuine and ethically grounded, they are more likely to engage, contribute meaningfully, and stay connected to a shared purpose. In my experience, the most effective leaders are those who lead with clarity as well as courage and heart.

Again, my experience is that leaders who lead with vulnerability are not weak but are leading with wisdom. When leaders speak openly about their limitations, share their mistakes, and genuinely seek to understand their teams, they create cultures of transparency and trust. McAdoo's[9] study, published in the *Open Journal of Business and Management*, reinforces this statement. It found that vulnerable leadership encourages authenticity and deeper interpersonal relationships. Drawing on Kanter's theory of structural empowerment, McAdoo showed that when leaders model humility and openness, employees perceive greater safety which strengthens fairness and trust. Fairness and trust are two pillars of strategic success and long-term engagement. Vulnerability, once avoided, is now recognised as a leadership strength that enhances connection, equity, and psychological safety.

---

9 McAdoo, J. (2025). The impact of vulnerable leadership on employee empowerment. *Open Journal of Business and Management*, 13(1), 1–23. https://doi.org/10.4236/ojbm.2025.131001

Affirmation and Recognition

I've come to believe that affirmation and recognition are essential elements of meaningful communication, not meant for human resource functions alone. Although Chapter 10, Recognition and Reward, is a detailed discussion that builds on the importance of affirmation and recognition in the workplace, I mention them here as a reminder of how they guide us to connect, communicate, and lead others.

In my experience, affirmation is one of the most powerful tools leaders have to foster genuine connection at work. It's not only about recognition; it's about seeing people, acknowledging their worth, and reinforcing their place in the team. Brené Brown's conversation with Dr. Laurie Santos on the *Dare to Lead* podcast beautifully captures this idea.[10] They explore how meaningful connection in the workplace is built through intentional practices like affirmation, empathy, and vulnerability. When we affirm others, we create a culture where people are valued, safe, and motivated to contribute authentically. That's the kind of leadership that transforms teams.

Recognition is a form of feedback, but it's also a form of care. Alexander Stajkovic and Fred

---

10   Brown, B. (Host). (2021, November 29). Brené with Dr. Laurie Santos on creating meaningful connection at work [Audio podcast episode]. In *Dare to Lead with Brené Brown*. Parcast Network.   https://brenebrown.com/podcast/creating-meaningful-connection-at-work/

Luthans[11] remind us that genuine appreciation, when expressed clearly and consistently, acts as a powerful natural reinforcer. Their meta-analysis showed that recognition alone improved service performance by 15 percent and, when paired with feedback, performance in manufacturing settings increased by up to 41 percent. It's striking that recognition had nearly the same impact as monetary rewards in manufacturing and twice the impact in service industries, which is a compelling case for its value as a cost-effective and universally applicable leadership tool.

The Chartered Institute of Personnel and Development adds further weight to the conversation about the importance of recognition and reward.[12] Their review of the evidence found that non-financial recognition has a moderate to significant positive effect on intrinsic motivation and performance, especially when it's personalised and unexpected. This taps into our innate human need to be seen and valued, a concept rooted in social comparison theory. Recognition, when relational and unconditional, strengthens morale,

---

11 Stajkovic, A. D., & Luthans, F. (2003). Behavioral management and task performance in organizations: Conceptual background, meta-analysis, and test of alternative models. Personnel Psychology, 56(1), 155–194. https://doi.org/10.1111/j.1744-6570.2003.tb00147.x

12 Cotton, C., Gifford, J., & Young, J. (2022). Incentives and recognition: An evidence review. Practice summary and recommendations. Chartered Institute of Personnel and Development. https://www.cipd.org/globalassets/media/knowledge/knowledge-hub/evidence-reviews/incentives-recognition-practice-summary_tcm18-105466.pdf

commitment, and engagement. In a contribution to the Harvard Business Review, Littlefield[13] takes this theory a step further with the concept of reflective recognition. Reflective recognition refers to leaders who make it a point to invite employees to share what they're proud of and why. This simple yet profound practice not only surfaces unseen efforts but also empowers individuals to reflect on their growth, a key driver of motivation. Employees who are well-recognised are over forty percent more engaged, more confident, and less likely to leave. In my view, recognition is more than a leadership strategy; recognition is a relational act that builds trust, belonging, and a culture of appreciation.

Visionary Storytelling

Communicating a compelling vision is one of the most generous acts of leadership. It's not merely about setting direction – it's about creating meaning. When leaders articulate a vision that connects individual roles to a larger purpose, they invite people into something bigger than themselves. As Choy[14] notes, a clear and meaningful vision helps employees understand both

---

13 Littlefield, C. (2022, October 25). A better way to recognize your employees. *Harvard Business Review.* https://hbr.org/2022/10/a-better-way-to-recognize-your-employees

14 Choy, E. K. (2025, February 9). Why leadership storytelling is actually so powerful. *Forbes.* https://www.forbes.com/sites/estherchoy/2025/02/09/why-leadership-storytelling-is-so-powerful/

what they're working on and *why* it matters. A sense of purpose generates belonging, significance, and deep engagement. When people see how their contributions align with a broader mission, they're more likely to commit, collaborate, and lead from where they are.

One of the most potent ways to bring vision to life is through storytelling. Stories humanise strategy.[15] They make abstract goals tangible and emotionally resonant. I like the example of Howard Schultz, former CEO of Starbucks, who used his personal story of growing up in public housing and witnessing his father's workplace injury to shape a leadership vision rooted in dignity and care. His storytelling wasn't just compelling – it was connective. It enabled employees to understand the *why* behind company policies and fostered a culture of shared values.

Similarly, Frei and Morriss[16] in their journal article for the *Harvard Business Review* show how storytelling enhances trust, emotional engagement, and motivation. It also allows leaders to demonstrate vulnerability and authenticity, two traits that strengthen relational bonds and psychological safety. When leaders share their own experiences, challenges, and lessons learned, they invite others to do the same. Openness creates a

---

15 O'Flaherty, S., Sanders, M. T., & Whillans, A. (2021, March 29). Research: A little recognition can provide a big morale boost. *Harvard Business Review.* https://hbr
16 Frei, F. X., & Morriss, A. (2023, November–December). Storytelling that drives bold change. *Harvard Business Review.* https://hbr.org/2023/11/storytelling-that-drives-bold-chang

culture where people are safe to take risks, innovate, and grow.

Ultimately, a compelling vision communicated through authentic storytelling transforms leadership from directive to inspirational. The shift from directive to inspirational highlights a movement from compliance to commitment. What I mean by this is that the focus moves from completing tasks as a tick-a-box requirement (compliance) to a mindset that engages with a task and an understanding of its meaning for the greater good (commitment).

PAUSE AND REFLECT

How do you foster increased connection?

- Do you communicate with clarity with compassion?

- Do you communicate with authenticity and vulnerability?

- Do you communicate with affirmation and recognition?

- Do you communicate with visionary storytelling?

- How is it possible to foster communication through showing compassion, vulnerability, giving recognition and storytelling?

Leadership That Lifts Others

Quality leadership lives in conversation with others. The way we speak and, more importantly, the intention behind our words shapes the culture we create. Research on communicative leadership reinforces this observation, showing that when leaders communicate with a genuine intention to connect and listen, employee engagement increases significantly.[17] It isn't merely about being available or responsive: it's about being relational. When employees perceive their leaders as truly communicative, trust grows and,

---

17 Kumar, S. S., Ku, B., Sen, R., Kumar, M., & Lata, R. (2024). Exploring the impact of communicative leadership on employee engagement: The mediated moderated effect of employee perceptions of communication and leaders' intention to use ChatGPT. *ResearchGate.* https://www.researchgate. net/publication/384205516_Exploring_the_Impact_of_ Communicative_Leadership_on_Employee_Engagement_ The_Mediated_Moderated_Effect_of_Employee_ Perceptions_of_Communication_and_Leaders'_Intention_ to_use_ChatGPT/fulltext/66ee7e16750edb3bea65de7f/ Exploring-the-Impact-of-Communicative-Leadership-on- Employee-Engagement-The-Mediated-Moderated-Effect- of-Employee-Perceptions-of-Communication-and-Leaders- Intention-to-use-ChatGPT.pdf

along with it, the willingness to contribute, collaborate, and commit. Adaptive, intentional communication is a strategic lever for performance and well-being.[18]

Communication as a strategic lever for performance and well-being is echoed in the work of Seppälä and McNichols,[19] who found that leaders who prioritise relationships and lead with kindness and authenticity consistently outperform their peers. Drawing on social psychology and self-determination theory, their research highlights emotional connection (feeling valued, respected, and understood) as the major driver of motivation and workplace success. What's particularly compelling is their finding that positive relationships at work are more influential than salary or benefits in determining employee well-being and engagement. It affirms what I see every day: when leaders speak to connect, they create environments where people are safe, seen, and supported. In these environments, people don't merely work, they thrive. Speaking to connect is the heartbeat of quality leadership, not simply a communication strategy.

---

18 Guthridge, L. (2025, April 18). How clear and explicit communication creates kind, compassionate and effective leaders. *Forbes.* https://www.forbes.com/councils/forbescoachescouncil/2025/04/18/how-clear-and-explicit-communication-creates-kind-compassionate-and-effective-leaders/
19 Seppälä, E., & McNichols, N. K. (2022, June 21). The power of healthy relationships at work. *Harvard Business Review.* https://hbr.org/2022/06/the-power-of-healthy-relationships-at-work

When leaders have well-developed communication skills, they are uniquely positioned to lift others as they lead by creating environments where people are valued, empowered, and inspired.[20] Effective communication goes beyond conveying information; it involves listening actively, expressing empathy, and adapting messages to meet the needs of diverse individuals.[21] Leaders who communicate clearly and compassionately support team members to understand their roles, expectations, and potential. Communicating with clarity reduces confusion and builds confidence, allowing employees to focus on growth and contribution rather than uncertainty or fear.[18]

The quality of today's leadership is deeply tied to the quality of conversation. Leaders who speak to connect cultivate trust, engagement, and a sense of belonging, all of which are essential for sustainable performance. This kind of communication requires presence, generosity, and intention.[22] To be **present, not passive** means showing up fully in conversations, listening deeply, and responding with

---

20 Rehkoph, F. (2025, March 12). 7 must know communication frameworks for leaders. *Falk Rehkopf.* https://falkrehkopf. com/7-must-know-communication-frameworks-for- leaders/
21 Brown, B. (2012). *Daring greatly: How the courage to be vulnerable transforms the way we live, love, parent, and lead.* Gotham Books.
22 Brown, B. (2018). *Dare to lead: Brave work, tough conversations, whole hearts.* Random House.

care. To **be generous, not jealous** is to celebrate others' contributions and create space for shared success. And to **be intentional, not incidental** is to lead with clarity and purpose, ensuring every interaction reinforces connection and alignment. Research consistently shows that relational communication strengthens emotional safety and motivation. When leaders embody these mantras, they don't merely manage, they inspire. Speaking to connect is not a technique: it's a commitment to lead with humanity and heart.

• • •

Takeaways

- Intentional communication builds trust.

- Emotional connection drives motivation.

- Relational leadership enhances engagement.

- Speaking to connect is a leadership imperative.

What will you START doing?

What will you CONTINUE doing?

What will you STOP doing?

Chapter Seven

Social Responsibility

I am of the opinion that my life belongs to the whole community and as long as I live, it is my privilege to do for it whatever I can. ~ George Bernard Shaw

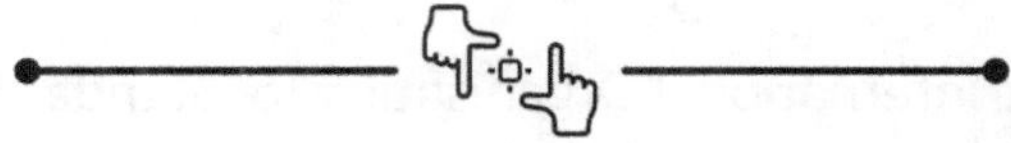

At Patagonia, a company renowned for its environmental activism, social responsibility is not just a policy, but a way of life that begins with its people. One of the most heartwarming initiatives is their Let My People Go Surfing policy, which encourages employees to take time off to enjoy nature, whether it's surfing, hiking, or volunteering. The initiative also fosters a sense of joy and value in their workplace. The company also provides on-site childcare, supports flexible schedules, and matches employee donations to environmental causes. This culture of care creates a joyful workplace where employees are valued for their work as well as for who they are as *individuals. It's a place where doing good for the planet and one another is simply part of the daily rhythm.*[1]

As leaders, we must recognise that social responsibility is not a fleeting trend. Now more than ever, it is a foundational principle of ethical leadership and sustainable organisational practice. It reflects our obligation, both individually and collectively, to act in ways that benefit society beyond our own interests. This responsibility is both moral and strategic, demanding that we remain accountable for the impact of our decisions on the environment, communities, and broader social systems. In doing so, we create the conditions for others to thrive and shape the future.

The International Organisation for Standardisation created the standard ISO 26000, which aims to motivate businesses and other organisations to engage in socially responsible practices with a conscious awareness and ownership of the impact of their decisions and activities on society and the environment.[2] Conscious awareness and ownership arise from transparent and ethical behaviour that supports sustainable development while honouring

---

1   Harnett, C. (2017, December 12). Let my people go surfing. *HR Executive.* https://hrexecutive.com/let-people-go-surfing/
2   International Organisation for Standardisation. (2010). ISO 26000: *Guidance on social responsibility.* ISO. https://www.iso.org/iso-26000-social-responsibility.html

stakeholder interests, laws, and international norms. An understanding of social responsibility emphasises leadership is about direction and stewardship. When leaders embrace the responsibility for stewardship, they model behaviours that elevate others and enable cultures of integrity and care.

Key human qualities to be cultured

Socially responsible leadership is underpinned by key human qualities that must be cultivated intentionally:

Key Human Qualities that Must be Cultured Intentionally

Empathy

Integrity

Sustainability

Community Engagement

- **Empathy** – the capacity to understand and value the experiences of others.

- **Integrity** – the commitment to act with honesty and consistency.

- **Sustainability** – the prioritisation of long-term ecological and social health.

- **Community Engagement** – the active building of inclusive, participatory environments.

These qualities are practical tools that guide decisions and behaviours, prioritising collective well-being over short-term personal or financial gain. Leaders who embody these qualities create ripple effects, empowering others to act with purpose and compassion.

In practice, social responsibility is visible across both community and corporate landscapes. At the grassroots level, it emerges through local clean-up drives, support for underprivileged groups, and the creation of inclusive public spaces.[3] Within organisations, it manifests through fair labour practices, diversity and inclusion programs, ethical sourcing, and corporate philanthropy. These are both policies and expressions of leadership that lift others.

Consider LEGO, which has committed over US$1.4 billion to sustainable materials (reducing single-use plastic and introducing paper-based bags)[4] as well as pursuing carbon neutral initiatives such as

---

3 Ferdman, B. M. (2021). Inclusive leadership: The fulcrum of inclusion. In B. M. Ferdman, J. Prime, & R. E. Riggio (Eds.), *Inclusive leadership: Transforming diverse lives, workplaces, and societies* (pp. 3–24). Routledge/Taylor & Francis Group. https://doi.org/10.4324/9780429449673-1

4 Mirza, Z. (2023, September 5). *Lego to invest $1.4B in sustainability as it pledges net-zero emissions by 2050.* ESG Dive. https://www.esgdive.com/news/lego-sustainability-investment-14b-net-zero-emissions-2050/693953/

new designs for factories and buildings, acquisition of renewable energy at its plants, offices and stores, and taking carbon dioxide emissions into account across all corporate decisions. This is leadership in action, where environmental stewardship becomes a platform for innovation and impact. Similarly, Starbucks integrates social responsibility through ethical sourcing and community store models that reinvest in local charities, building trust and fostering a culture of shared responsibility.[5] These examples illustrate how socially responsible leadership can transform business into a force for good.

Ultimately, when leaders embrace social responsibility, they do more than meet ethical standards because they create environments where others can rise. I maintain that the essence of leadership is not to stand above others, but to lift them metaphorically through principled action, shared values, and a commitment to the greater good.

It is through socially responsible leadership that we create the conditions for others to rise. When we act with integrity, empathy, and foresight, our leading transforms into lifting. Social responsibility is the mechanism by which leadership becomes transformational, shaping both organisational

---

5 Dudovskiy, J. (2022, October 8). Starbucks CSR: Corporate social responsibility. *Research-Methodology.* https:// research-methodology.net/starbucks-csr-corporate-social-responsibility/

outcomes as well as societal progress.[6] This transformative power of leadership should inspire us to act with purpose and commitment to the greater good.

PAUSE AND REFLECT

What do you do in your workplace that exemplifies social responsibility?

The connection between leadership and social responsibility is deeply rooted in theory. Stakeholder theory, transformational leadership, and Upper Echelons theory all provide robust frameworks for understanding how leaders can and must act in ways that benefit the wider community. These theories remind us that leadership is not about control: it is about contribution.

Stakeholder theory, first proposed by R. Edward Freeman in the 1980s, asserts that leaders must consider the interests of all stakeholders – not

---

6 Ayoko, O. B. (2022). Leadership, ethics and corporate social responsibility. *Journal of Management & Organization*, 28(1), 1–8. https://doi.org/10.1017/jmo.2022.13

only shareholders – in their decision-making.[7] This theory challenges us to expand our ethical lens and recognise our responsibility to employees, customers, suppliers, communities, and the environment. Unilever exemplifies this approach through its *Sustainable Living Plan*, which integrates stakeholder needs into every strategic decision. By reducing environmental impact while improving health and well-being, Unilever demonstrates how socially responsible leadership can create shared value. It is this shared value that supports leadership that lifts.

In my workshops, I often speak about the transformative power of leadership theories. Leaders who embrace transformational principles drive innovation, ethical behaviour, and a deep commitment to corporate social responsibility (CSR). According to Mansaray and Atan,[8] transformational leadership significantly enhances CSR outcomes through inspirational motivation, individualised consideration, and vision-sharing. Their study of public universities in Sierra Leone revealed that such leaders catalyse community outreach, sustainability projects, and

---

7　Simon, B. (2023, August 4). What is stakeholder theory and how does it impact an organization? *Smartsheet*. https://www. smartsheet.com/what-stakeholder-theory-and-how-does-it-impact-organization

8　Mansaray, I., & Atan, T. (2025). Exploring corporate social responsibility: The role of transformational leadership, innovative work behavior, and organizational culture in public universities of Sierra Leone. *Sustainability*, 17(17), 7653. https://doi.org/10.3390/su17177653

ethical education programs. This is leadership that lifts by cultivating cultures of responsibility and collaboration.

Although it is less commonly discussed, Upper Echelons theory offers critical insights into how the personal attributes of top leaders shape organisational outcomes, including CSR initiatives.[9] Lee et al.[10] found that factors such as age, education and tenure influence how leaders perceive stakeholder needs and societal expectations. CEOs with longer tenure and broader engagement tend to implement more socially responsible practices, particularly in areas like community involvement and environmental sustainability. The Upper Echelons theory reinforces the idea that, as leaders, our values, experiences, and perspectives directly impact our capacity to lift others through socially responsible action.

At the heart of all these theories lies ethical leadership. Research consistently shows that CEOs and senior executives set the tone for ethical conduct and sustainability.[5] The commitment of CEOs and senior executives determines whether CSR efforts are superficial or deeply embedded. Ethical leadership

---

9 Liu, X. (2023). A literature review of upper echelons theory. *In SHS Web of Conferences* (Vol. 169, p. 01067). EDP Sciences.

10 Lee, W. S., Sun, K. A., & Moon, J. (2017). Application of upper echelon theory for corporate social responsibility dimensions: Evidence from the restaurant industry. *Journal of Quality Assurance in Hospitality & Tourism.* https://doi.org/10.1080/1528008X.2017.1421492

theory highlights the importance of moral reasoning, fairness, and accountability.[11] Leaders who act with integrity build trust and legitimacy, both within and beyond the organisation. The Body Shop stands as a beacon of ethical leadership, promoting cruelty-free products and fair trade. Its leaders embed ethics into every aspect of the business from sourcing to employee treatment.[12] This is leadership that lifts by aligning values with action.

Socially responsive considerations

Socially-responsive leaders foster a workplace that is inclusive, culturally responsive, and reflective of community engagement.[13]

11 Wang, Z., Ye, Y., & Liu, X. (2024). How CEO responsible leadership shapes corporate social responsibility and organization performance: The roles of organizational climates and CEO founder status. *International Journal of Contemporary Hospitality Management*, 36(6), 1944–1962. https://doi.org/10.1108/IJCHM-11-2022-149

12 Magnifico. (2023, September 30). The Body Shop: Ethical beauty, empowering communities, and environmental stewardship. *We Are Magnifico*. https://www.wearemagnifico.com/post/the-body-shop-ethical-beauty-empowering-communities-and-environmental-stewardship

13 Peters, H. C., Luke, M., Bernard, J., & Trepal, H. (2020). Socially just and culturally responsive leadership within counseling and counseling psychology: A grounded theory investigation. *The Counseling Psychologist*, 48(7), 953–985. https://doi.org/10.1177/0011000020937431

Socially Responsive Considerations:
Inclusive, Culturally Responsive and Ethical Action

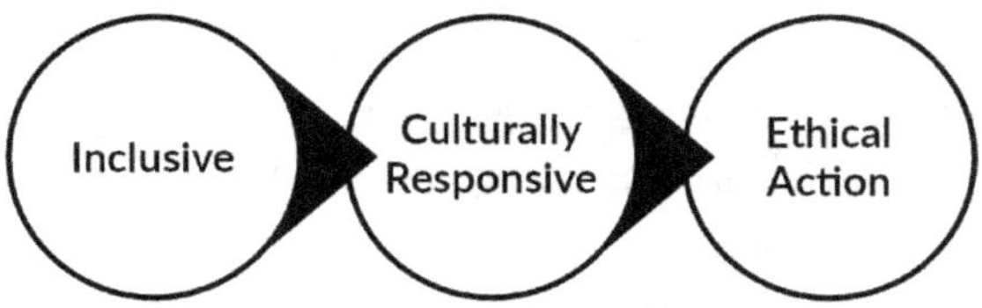

Figure 7.1: Source: N. Bonfiglio-Pavisich, © (2025).

As leaders, our role is not simply to lead. It is to elevate. To progress inclusion, we must ensure that every individual within our organisation is valued, respected, and empowered to contribute. This requires more than good intentions; it demands deliberate action. Inclusive leadership involves equitable hiring practices, cultivating diverse leadership pipelines, and embedding inclusive language and behaviours into daily interactions. These strategies promote a positive work culture and employee satisfaction and lead to increased innovation and better decision-making. Leaders must create safe spaces for feedback via anonymous surveys, listening sessions, and employee resource groups that are powerful tools for reflecting the diversity of our workforce. Inclusion is the active practice of accountability and care.[3] When we lead inclusively, we lift others by creating environments where everyone can thrive.

Cultural responsiveness is equally essential. Being culturally responsive means adapting leadership and organisational practices to reflect the lived realities of our employees, clients, and communities. It requires us to recognise that communication styles, decision-making preferences, and expressions of respect vary across cultures. Leaders must seek input from culturally diverse stakeholders and tailor policies to be both sensitive and relevant. For example, adjusting meeting formats to accommodate different communication norms or celebrating cultural holidays that reflect team diversity are acts of respect, not symbolic gestures. Such responsiveness builds trust, strengthens relationships both internally and externally, and fosters security and confidence.[13] In doing so, leaders lift others by honouring their identities and experiences.

In my leadership workshops, I emphasise how leaders can initiate community engagement. Community engagement is a powerful avenue through which leaders extend their influence beyond the workplace. By building partnerships with local organisations, supporting volunteer initiatives, and aligning business goals with community needs, leaders create shared value. These actions enhance the organisation's reputation, but more importantly they demonstrate that leadership is about contribution, not control. A leader who encourages employees to participate in community service or integrates social impact into strategic planning is modelling a philosophy of service.[14] This is leadership that lifts others. It does so by connecting organisations to the communities they serve.

PAUSE AND REFLECT

What do you do to be inclusive, culturally responsive and ethical in your actions at work?

Leadership education is evolving to reflect inclusive, culturally-responsive, and community-engaged approaches as imperatives to leadership development. This kind of initiative includes teaching future leaders to value collaboration, equity, and civic duty. Programs that emphasise ethical decision-making, social justice, and sustainability prepare leaders to navigate complex societal challenges. Importantly, socially-responsible leadership is not confined to corporate settings. It applies across sectors, including

---

14 Viola, J. J., Olson, B. D., Reed, S. F., Jimenez, T. R., & Smith, C. M. (2015). Building and strengthening collaborative community partnerships. In V. C. Scott & S. M. Wolfe (Eds.), *Community psychology: Foundations for practice* (pp. 237–261). Sage Publications. https://doi.org/10.4135/9781483398150.n9

education, healthcare, government, and nonprofits. The goal is to cultivate leaders who lift others by creating environments where people and communities can flourish.[15]

Lifting others through leadership requires a deep commitment to social responsibility. Leaders who prioritise fairness, opportunity, and well-being use their influence to foster trust and psychological safety. When employees observe that their organisation values people over profits, they are more likely to engage, innovate, and remain committed. Inclusive hiring practices and support for employee well-being are human resource strategies that embody expressions of care. Externally, socially-responsible leaders build bridges with communities and stakeholders, advocate for environmental stewardship, and support local initiatives. These actions create ripple effects of positive change.[16]

Shemara Wikramanayake, CEO of Macquarie Group, exemplifies this philosophy. As the first woman and first Asian-Australian to lead an ASX 200 company, her leadership is marked by both financial success and a profound commitment to environmental and social responsibility. Under her guidance, Macquarie has become one of the world's largest investors in renewable

---

15 Nemerowicz, G., & Rossi, E. (2014). *Education for leadership and social responsibility*. Routledge.

16 Harvey, M. (2020). First but not last: Australian women who have gone first. *Redress, 29*(2), 25–27.

energy, actively supporting the global transition to a low-carbon economy. She has championed climate change mitigation, sustainable infrastructure, and ethical investment practices, positioning Macquarie as a leader in responsible capitalism. Her advocacy for diversity and inclusion within the organisation further reflects her belief in representation and equity. Wikramanayake's leadership demonstrates how social responsibility can be embedded into a core business strategy of lifting others by creating opportunity, promoting sustainability, and driving systemic change.

Leaders who embrace social responsibility play a transformative role in shaping ethical, inclusive, and purpose-driven environments. By prioritising values such as equity, sustainability, and community engagement, they inspire others to act with integrity and compassion. Their influence extends beyond organisational boundaries, facilitating cultures where collaboration and civic duty thrive.[17] Such leaders model ethical decision-making and empower teams to contribute meaningfully to society. Whether in business, education, healthcare, or government, socially responsible leadership creates ripple effects, uplifting individuals, strengthening communities, and driving long-term positive change. The transformative power

---

17   Chief Executives Council. (2024, February 15). Ethical leadership and social responsibility. https://chiefexecutivescouncil.org/ethical-leadership-and-social-responsibility

of socially responsible leadership is both inspiring and a call to action for all leaders.

Let me be clear: socially responsible leadership is a necessity. It's not something we add on when it's convenient; it's a foundational capability that defines how we show up, how we lead, and how we serve. When leaders lead with empathy, integrity, and vision, they don't just drive outcomes, they create the conditions for people, communities, and organisations to thrive.

We know from both research and lived experience that leadership is no longer merely about strategy and execution. It's about connection, recognition, and authenticity. The most impactful leaders are those who foster psychological safety, trust, and belonging, whether through reflective recognition, storytelling, or the courage to lead with vulnerability. But this kind of leadership doesn't happen by accident. It begins with a conscious choice: the commitment to show up differently. It starts when we choose to **be present, not passive.** Presence is about more than being in the room. It's about being fully engaged, listening deeply, and responding with care. It's about noticing what's not being said and creating space for others to be seen and heard.

Social responsibility continues when we choose to **be generous, not jealous.** Generosity in leadership means lifting others, sharing credit, and celebrating success without comparison. It's a mindset of abundance – one that builds trust, strengthens relationships, and enhances collective growth. And it's sustained when we choose to **be intentional, not incidental.** Social responsibility in leadership is not a by-product; it's a deliberate practice. It requires clarity of purpose, consistency in action, and a deep commitment to values that prioritise people over ego, and long-term impact over short-term gain. These may seem like subtle shifts, but their impact is profound. They shape the culture we create, the well-being we protect, and the legacy we leave behind.

• • •

Takeaways

- Social responsibility is a catalyst for lifting others.

- Inclusion requires intentional leadership.

- Cultural responsiveness builds trust.

- Community engagement extends leadership impact.

- Leadership education must embrace social responsibility.

What will you START doing?

What will you CONTINUE doing?

What will you STOP doing?

Chapter Eight

Conflict Intelligence

The quality of our lives depends not on whether or not we have conflicts, but on how we respond to them. ~ Thomas Crum

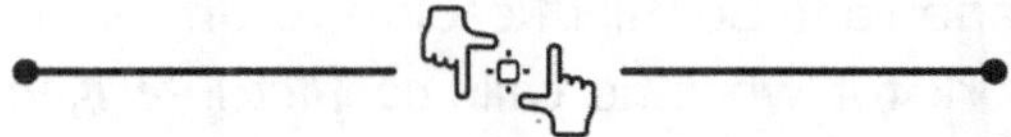

At a community-based nonprofit focused on youth empowerment, the executive director, Maya, leads with a commitment to healthy conflict. Her team meets weekly in structured sessions designed to encourage open dialogue. Everybody's voice is heard and respected. Maya sets clear boundaries for communication: they are active listening, no interruptions, and feedback framed around shared goals. Disagreements are welcomed as opportunities for growth, not threats to harmony. Team members are psychologically safe to challenge ideas, knowing their perspectives matter. Over time, this communicational culture has fostered deep trust, stronger collaboration, *and innovative solutions to complex social issues. Maya's leadership proves that when conflict is led well, it becomes a force for unity and impact.*

Let's be clear: conflict is not a problem to be solved: it's a reality to be led through. As Amy Gallo[1] reminds us, conflict is inevitable. What matters is how we show up in it. In today's increasingly polarised workplaces, leaders must do more than manage conflict; they must master it.

Peter Coleman,[2] a contributor to *Harvard Business Review* and a leading researcher at Columbia University's Morton Deutsch International Centre for Cooperation and Conflict Resolution, offers a powerful framework for what he calls *conflict intelligence.* Yes, conflict intelligence is about resolving disputes but it's more than that: it's about leading through complexity with clarity and courage. Coleman identifies four core competencies that every leader must cultivate:

- **Self-awareness and self-regulation** – Know your triggers. Manage your emotions. Lead yourself first.

---

1   Gallo, A. (2022). *Getting along: How to work with anyone (even difficult people).* Harvard Business Review Press.
2   Coleman, P. T. (2025, July–August). The conflict-intelligent leader. *Harvard Business Review.* https://hbr.org/2025/07/the-conflict-intelligent-leader

- **Social-conflict skills** – Listen deeply. Communicate clearly. Build trust.

- **Situational adaptivity** – Read the room. Flex your approach. Stay agile.

- **Systemic wisdom** – Understand the bigger picture. Address root causes. Lead change, not just conversations.

When leaders develop these competencies, they shift the focus from reducing tension to creating environments where psychological safety, creativity, and collaboration thrive. Conflict intelligence is the leader's capacity to turn conflict into a catalyst for growth.[3] Doing so requires healthy conflict.

Alan Mulally: A Case Study in Conflict-Intelligent Leadership

Look at Alan Mulally's transformation of Ford Motor Company.[4] In 2006, Ford was drowning in a toxic culture of silos, blame, and fear. Executives avoided bad news and meetings were battlegrounds. Mulally did more than change the strategy: he changed the

---

3 Coleman, P. T. (2018). Conflict intelligence and systemic wisdom: Meta-competencies for engaging conflict in a complex, dynamic world. *Negotiation Journal*, 34(1), 7–35. https://doi.org/10.1111/nejo

4 Warrick, D. D., & Mulally, A. (2024). The leadership principles Alan Mulally followed in transforming Ford Motor Company into a successful company with a strong people-oriented culture. In *Cases on Critical Leadership Skills* (pp. 120–133). Edward Elgar Publishing.

conversation. He introduced weekly Business Plan Review meetings where leaders were encouraged to speak openly, without fear of blame. His mantra? "So-and-so has a problem. He's not the problem. Who can support him with that?"[5] That's conflict intelligence in action. Shifting the focus from fault to solution and from isolation to collaboration.

Mulally's *One Ford* vision broke down silos and aligned global teams under a shared purpose. His leadership was rooted in transparency, emotional intelligence, and data-driven decision-making.[6] These qualities guided Ford to weather the 2008 financial crisis without a government bailout. That is more than smart leadership: it is courageous leadership.

Redefining Conflict: From Threat to Opportunity

Let's redefine what conflict means in leadership. Healthy conflict is about contribution, not confrontation. Healthy conflict occurs in a space where diverse perspectives meet, assumptions are challenged, and

---

5   Edmondson, A. C., & Jung, O. (2021). The turnaround at Ford Motor Company (Rev. ed., August 2024). *Harvard Business School Case* 621-101. https://www.hbs.edu/faculty/Pages/item.aspx?num=59955

6   Hoffman, B. G. (2012, March 12). Saving an iconic brand: Five ways Alan Mulally changed Ford's culture. *Fast Company.* https://www.fastcompany.com/1680075/saving-an-ic

better decisions are made. Healthy conflict is respectful, open, and solution focused.[7] It's not about winning: it's about learning. Healthy conflict is not about being right: it's about getting it right. When leaders embrace healthy conflict, they unlock the full potential of their teams.

So, the question isn't, "How do I avoid conflict?" The question is, "How do I lead through it?" Step up. Lean in. Lead forward.

Let's get one thing straight: if you're leading a team and avoiding conflict, you're not leading. In fact, what you are doing is trying to manage comfort. Patrick Lencioni's work reminds us that healthy conflict is a necessity, not a disruption.[8] High-performing teams don't shy away from disagreement. They lean into it with purpose. Lencioni outlines three truths every leader must embrace:

Conflict is Necessary for Commitment and Results

Artificial harmony is the enemy of progress. When team members are safe to challenge ideas, they're

---

7 Taylor, S. (2024, April 2). Why leaders should embrace healthy conflict in the workplace. *Forbes Business Council*. https://www.forbes.com/councils/forbesbusinesscouncil/2024/04/02/why-leaders-should-embrace-healthy-conflict-in-the-workplace/

8 Lencioni, P. (2002). *The five dysfunctions of a team: A leadership fable*. Jossey-Bass.

more likely to commit to decisions, even those they initially resisted. Why? Because they were heard.

Conflict Builds Trust

Vulnerability is the foundation of trust. When people can admit mistakes, speak openly, and disagree respectfully, trust deepens. Trust is the soil where healthy conflict grows.

Conflict Drives Innovation and Better Decisions

Leaders must mine for conflict and not suppress it. Diverse viewpoints challenge assumptions, prevent groupthink, and lead to smarter, more inclusive decisions.

PAUSE AND REFLECT

How do you turn up in a conflict situation at work?

Healthy Conflict: A Leadership Imperative That Lifts

In my workshops, I repeatedly emphasise that leadership is no longer defined by authority alone. It is defined by the capacity to elevate others through intentional, values-driven action. One of the most powerful yet often misunderstood tools in a leader's toolkit is healthy conflict. Far from being disruptive, healthy conflict is a catalyst for growth, innovation, and resilience. Leaders create environments where respectful dissent is welcomed, emotional intelligence is modelled, and psychological safety is protected by unlocking the full potential of their teams.[9] I emphasise that this is not about managing tension; on the contrary, it's about transforming it into opportunity. When embedded into culture and guided by ethical leadership, healthy conflict becomes a mechanism for lifting individuals, strengthening teams, and aligning organisations with purpose.

---

9 Coleman, P. T. (2012). Constructive conflict resolution and sustainable peace. In P. T. Coleman & M. Deutsch (Eds.), *Psychological components of sustainable peace* (pp. 55–84). Springer. https://doi.org/10.1007/978-1-4614-3555-6_3

Healthy Conflict

Figure 8.1

Healthy Conflict in Action

In practice, healthy conflict transforms workplace conversations. It turns routine meetings into dynamic exchanges where ideas are challenged constructively. For example, when a team member questions a timeline based on past experience and that challenge is welcomed and not dismissed, it leads to better planning, stronger outcomes, and deeper engagement.

But this process doesn't happen by accident. It requires intentional leadership. Leaders must model emotional regulation, active listening, and open-mindedness. They should also create structures such as feedback loops and regular check-ins that normalise disagreement and reward respectful dissent.

The Ripple Effect on Team Dynamics

I will speak more about team dynamics in Chapter 9, but I do want to mention the concept here in terms of healthy conflict. When teams engage in healthy conflict, they become more resilient. The team learns to navigate tension without tearing one another apart. It clarifies roles, sharpens priorities, and builds mutual respect. Over time, the team becomes more engaged, more innovative, and more aligned.[10] This approach to team dynamics also connects with a style of leadership that lifts others. By sustaining environments where challenge is not feared but embraced, the ripple effect forms a collective pathway to excellence.

Conflict as a Catalyst for Innovation

Innovation doesn't come from agreement. It comes from friction. When ideas collide, new possibilities emerge. In product development, for instance, conflicting views

---

10 O'Neill, T. A., & McLarnon, M. J. W. (2018). Optimizing team conflict dynamics for high performance teamwork. *Human Resource Management Review*, 28(4), 378–394. https://doi.org/10.1016/j.hrmr.2017.06.002

on user needs can spark deeper research and lead to breakthrough design. Leaders who foster this kind of dialogue are positioning their teams to adapt, evolve, and lead.[11] Healthy conflict, when guided with purpose, becomes a strategic advantage.

Emotions Matter: So Lead Them

Even healthy conflict can stir emotions. That's normal. What matters is how leaders respond. Acknowledge the emotion. Validate the concern. Then guide the conversation back to shared goals. Emotional intelligence, no longer considered a soft skill, is a leadership imperative.[12] Leaders who lift others do so by recognising the emotional landscape of their teams and responding with empathy and clarity.

When Conflict Turns Toxic

Not all conflict is productive. When it becomes personal, hostile, or avoidant, it erodes trust and morale. In my first book in the Show Up and Lead series, *It's All About*

---

11 Harvard Business Publishing. (2024). Why conflict is the key to unlocking innovation. https://www.harvardbusiness.org/insight/why-conflict-is-the-key-to-unlocking-innovation

12 Babatunde, F., Sunday, H., & Adeshina, O. (2023). Emotional intelligence in conflict management and leadership effectiveness in organizations. *International Journal of Research*, 10(3), 146–150. https://www.researchgate.net/publication/369538702_Emotional_Intelligence_in_Conflict_Management_and_Leadership_Effectiveness_in_Organization

It![13] I insist that conflict should focus on the behaviour or the action and never the person. For this to occur, it requires all of us – including leaders – to adopt a curious, responsive and doing mindset. Leaders should spot the signs of passive aggression, withdrawal, repeated misunderstandings and intervene early. Mediation, clear norms, and courageous conversations are key to restoring psychological safety.[14] Leadership that lifts is proactive, not reactive, and it addresses toxicity before it takes root.

Embedding Healthy Conflict into Culture

Practices have to be embedded into the workplace culture to sustain healthy conflict. Such practices include celebrating constructive dissent, training teams in conflict resolution, and modelling how to disagree productively.[15] When leaders consistently lift others through respectful engagement, they create workplaces that are inclusive, agile, and aligned. Culture

---

13   Bonfiglio-Pavisich, N. (2024). *It's all about IT!: Evidence-based, practical guide to workplace communications.* Turtle Publishing.

14   Normore, A., Javidi, M., & Long, L. (Eds.). (2019). *Handbook of research on strategic communication, leadership, and conflict management in modern organizations.* Business Science Reference/IGI Global. https://doi.org/10.4018/978-1-5225-8516-9

15   Rechter, N. (2024). Conflict resolution and its role in organizational culture. *Journal of Organizational Culture, Communications and Conflict, 28*(S3), 1–3. https://www.abacademies.org/articles/conflict-resolution-and-its-role-in-organizational-culture-17070.html

becomes the container for courageous conversations and, of course, the playground for healthy conflict.

Understanding Conflict Archetypes: Leading with Insight

Here's where Amy Gallo's[1] conflict archetypes become essential. Not all conflict looks the same because not all people engage with conflict the same way. Gallo offers eight coworker archetypes that may be deemed as difficult and offers strategies to constructively work with each one. Examples of the archetypes include: the Passive-Aggressive, the Know-It-All, the Avoider, and the Pleaser. Gallo's message is clear: relationships matter. Understanding these archetypes enables leaders to tailor their approach. I've made this point already, however it bears repeating: the issue or behaviour, not the people, is what healthy conflict is about. When leaders recognise the behavioural patterns behind the tension, they are better able to shift from reacting to leading. That's the difference between managing conflict and mastering it.

Leading Through Conflict: Styles and Strategy

To lead effectively, we must understand the different ways people engage with conflict and how those styles shape team dynamics, decision-making, and culture. In my book, *It's All About It!*[16] I explored the Thomas-Kilmann Conflict Mode Instrument,[17] which uses assertiveness and cooperativeness to define five conflict styles: avoiding, accommodating, competing, compromising, and collaborating. The higher the assertiveness and cooperativeness, the more collaboration is evident in a conflict situation. The Thomas-Killman instrument helps leaders identify their own style and adapt to the needs of others.[18]

Gallo's conflict archetypes complement this model by offering behavioural insights. For example, assigning the Pessimist a formal role as a devil's advocate channels their risk-awareness constructively. Managing the Know-It-All involves setting boundaries and inviting diverse input to balance dominance. Leaders avoid labelling people by using these strategies to lead with insight and compassion.

---

16 Bonfiglio-Pavisich, N. (2024). *It's all about IT!: Evidence-based, practical guide to workplace communications.* Turtle Publishing.

17 Thomas, K. W., & Kilmann, R. H. (1974). *Thomas-Kilmann Conflict Mode Instrument* (TKI) [Database record]. PsycTESTS. https://doi.org/10.1037/t02326-000

18 Thomas, K. W. (1992). Conflict and conflict management. In J. W. Newstrom & K. Davis (Eds.), *Organizational behavior: Human behavior at work* (9th ed.). McGraw-Hill.

Fostering Healthy Conflict in the Workplace: Key Concepts for Constructive Engagement

Healthy conflict is a vital component of a thriving workplace. It allows individuals and teams to engage in meaningful dialogue, challenge ideas, and co-create solutions without fear or hostility. For conflict to be productive rather than destructive, eight foundational elements must be present (Fig. 8.2). These include psychological safety, emotional intelligence, constructive communication, collaboration, clarity of roles, a feedback culture, conflict resolution skills, and shared values. Together, these elements create an environment where conflict becomes a catalyst for growth, innovation, and stronger relationships. Let's go through and explore these in the context of the workplace.

Foundational Elements for Productive Conflict

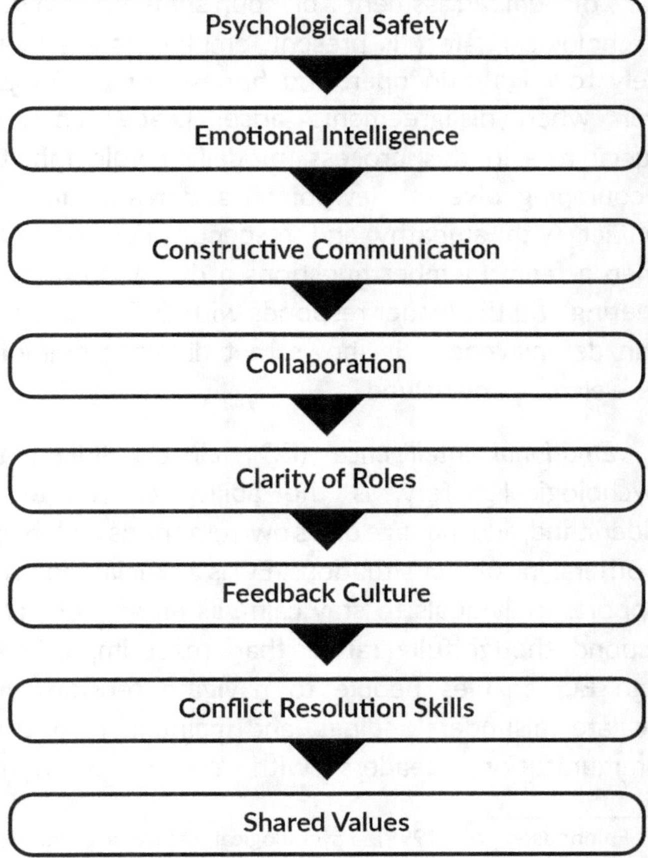

Figure 8.2: Source: N. Bonfiglio-Pavisich, © (2025).

Psychological safety, the cornerstone of healthy conflict, is a concept that leaders can actively pursue. It refers to an environment where individuals are safe to speak up, share ideas, and challenge others without fear of embarrassment or punishment.[19] When psychological safety is present, employees are more likely to engage in open and honest conversations, even when disagreements arise. Leaders play a crucial role in this process, modelling vulnerability, encouraging diverse viewpoints, and responding to conflict with empathy and respect.[20] For example, when a team member questions a decision during a meeting and the leader responds with curiosity rather than defensiveness, it shows that differing opinions are welcome and valued.

Emotional intelligence (EQ), closely linked to psychological safety, is the ability to recognise, understand, and manage one's own emotions and those of others. In conflict situations, EQ is a crucial tool that supports individuals to stay calm, listen actively, and respond thoughtfully rather than react impulsively. High EQ enables people to navigate tension, de-escalate misunderstandings, and maintain respectful communication. Leaders with strong emotional

---

19 Edmondson, A. (1999). Psychological safety and learning behavior in work teams. *Administrative Science Quarterly*, 44(2), 350–383. https://doi.org/10.2307/2666999
20 Kim, S., Lee, H., & Connerton, T. P. (2020). How psychological safety affects team performance: Mediating role of efficacy and learning behavior. *Frontiers in Psychology*, 11, Article 1581. https://doi.org/10.3389/fpsyg.2020.01581

intelligence can guide teams through conflict with clarity and compassion, turning disagreements into opportunities for growth.[21] For instance, a manager who notices rising tension between colleagues might intervene with empathy, helping both parties are heard and understood.

Constructive communication (Fig. 8.2) is a vital element of healthy conflict. It involves transparent, respectful, and solution-oriented dialogue. This includes using I statements, asking clarifying questions, and focusing on behaviours or outcomes rather than personal traits. Constructive communication prevents defensiveness and keeps the conversation focused on resolving the issue.[9] It also involves active listening, paraphrasing, and validating others' perspectives, all of which builds trust and mutual understanding.[22] For example, instead of saying, "You're always late", a colleague might say, "I've noticed delays in our meetings. Can we talk about what's causing them?".

Rather than viewing conflict as a win-lose scenario, healthy conflict encourages *collaboration* and problem-solving. Although I recognise this is not an

---

21 Gukssa, A. (2023). Role of emotional intelligence in conflict resolution strategies. *International Journal of Human Resource*, 1(1), 13–23.

22 Peterson, R. S., & Ferguson, A. J. (2014). Strategies for developing trust through constructive conflict resolution in teams. In O. B. Ayoko, N. M. Ashkanasy, & K. A. Jehn (Eds.), *Handbook of conflict management research* (pp. 193–204). Edward Elgar Publishing. https://doi.org/10.4337/9781781006948.00020

easy process, working together to identify root causes, explore options, and co-create solutions is critical to sharing opposing opinions.[23] Collaborative problem-solving fosters shared ownership and strengthens team cohesion. It also allows for more innovative and inclusive outcomes as diverse perspectives are integrated into the decision-making process. For example, when two departments disagree on resource allocation, a collaborative leader might facilitate a joint planning session to align priorities and find a balanced solution.

Clarity of roles and expectations is another critical factor in preventing and managing conflict. Many workplace disagreements stem from unclear responsibilities or misaligned goals.[24] Healthy conflict is supported by clarity, when everyone understands their scope of work, decision-making authority, and performance standards that have been established in team norms. Leaders can prevent unnecessary conflict by setting clear goals, communicating openly, and revisiting expectations regularly. When conflict

---

23 Altaras, A., Nikitović, T., Mojović Zdravković, K., Krstić, K., Rajić, M., Pavlović Babić, D., & Jolić Marjanović, Z. (2025). The role of emotional intelligence in collaborative problem solving: A systematic review. *Canadian Psychology / Psychologie canadienne*, 66(1), 45–67. https://doi.org/10.1037/cap0000401

24 Lacerenza, C. N., Marlow, S. L., Tannenbaum, S. I., & Salas, E. (2018). Team development interventions: Evidence-based approaches for improving teamwork. *American Psychologist*, 73(4), 517–531. https://doi.org/10.1037/amp0000295

does arise, clarity enables teams to focus on facts and solutions rather than assumptions or blame.

A strong *feedback culture* also contributes to healthy conflict (Fig. 8.2). When feedback is normalised and delivered respectfully, conflict becomes less threatening and more productive.[25] Employees learn to view feedback as a tool for improvement rather than criticism. Leaders who model and encourage feedback help teams build resilience and adaptability, making conflict a natural part of learning and development.[26] For example, regular team retrospectives that include open discussions about what worked and what didn't encourage tensions to surface and be resolved before they escalate.

To navigate conflict effectively, individuals and teams must also develop *conflict resolution skills* such as negotiation, mediation, and de-escalation. These skills manage tension, find common ground, and move

---

25 Hartmann, S., Weiss, M., Newman, A., & Hoegl, M. (2020). Resilience in the workplace: A multilevel review and synthesis. *Applied Psychology: An International Review*, 69(3), 913–959. https://doi.org/10.1111/apps.12191

26 Salas, E., Salazar, M. R., Feitosa, J., & Kramer, W. S. (2014). Collaboration and conflict in work teams. In B. Schneider & K. M. Barbera (Eds.), *The Oxford handbook of organizational climate and culture* (pp. 382–399). Oxford University Press. https://doi.org/10.1093/oxfordhb/9780199860715.013.0020

towards resolution.[27] Training in conflict resolution equips employees and leaders to handle disagreements confidently and constructively. It also reduces the likelihood of escalation and promotes a culture of accountability and respect.[28] For instance, a team lead trained in mediation might support two colleagues in resolving a disagreement by steering them through a structured conversation focused on shared goals.

The final element in Figure 8.2, *shared values* and *purpose*, provides a unifying framework for conflict resolution. When teams are aligned around shared values and a clear mission, disagreements are easier to navigate. Conflict is seen in the context of collective goals, which helps maintain focus and unity. Leaders can reinforce shared values by connecting conflict resolution to the organisation's purpose, reminding teams that healthy debate is part of achieving meaningful outcomes.[29] For example, in a healthcare organisation, a disagreement about resource allocation

27 Ngcobo, M. T. (2024). Navigating the emotional landscape of mediation: An exploration of the role of emotions in conflict resolution and the strategies for effective management. *Conflict Resolution Quarterly*, 41(3), 327–335. https://doi.org/10.1002/crq.21409

28 Accinni, T., Papadogiannis, G., & Orso, L. (2021). De-escalation techniques in various settings. In Empathy, Normalization and De-escalation: *Management of the Agitated Patient in Emergency and Critical Situations* (pp. 65–91). Cham: Springer International Publishing.

29 Bradley, B. H., Anderson, H. J., Baur, J. E., & Klotz, A. C. (2015). When conflict helps: Integrating evidence for beneficial conflict in groups and teams under three perspectives. *Group Dynamics: Theory, Research, and Practice*, 19(4), 243.

might be resolved by asking, "What decision best serves our patients?".

Healthy conflict is not a disruption to leadership. It is a demonstration of it. It is both possible and essential for organisational success. When leaders cultivate the elements of psychological safety, emotional intelligence, constructive communication, collaboration, clarity, feedback, conflict resolution skills, and shared values (Fig. 8.2), they transform conflict into a powerful force for progress. Teams are empowered to engage openly, solve problems creatively, and build resilient workplaces. When leadership practices lift others, leaders focus on **being present, not passive** because, instead of avoiding discomfort, they show up with courage and clarity.

When leaders embrace conflict as a space for contribution rather than confrontation, they foster cultures of trust, agility, and innovation. They lift others by validating emotion, encouraging diverse perspectives, and guiding teams towards shared goals. But engaging in healthy conflict requires consistency and conviction. It means intervening when conflict turns toxic, embedding respectful disagreement into daily practice, and modelling emotional intelligence as a leadership imperative. As leaders who lift others, **be generous, not jealous,** because collaboration thrives when we celebrate others. And don't forget to **be intentional, not incidental** because great leadership is never accidental; it's a choice made moment by moment.

. . .

Takeaways

- Trust and vulnerability.

- Focus on issues, not personalities.

- Shared goals and values.

- Clear norms and boundaries.

- Leader facilitation.

What will you START doing?

What will you CONTINUE doing?

What will you STOP doing?

Chapter Nine

Team Dynamics: The Engine of Modern Leadership

Alone we can do so little; together we can do so much. ~ Helen Keller

World Central Kitchen (WCK) was founded by chef José Andrés. During natural disasters and humanitarian crises, WCK mobilises rapidly to deliver meals to affected communities, often under extreme conditions. The team operates with clear roles, shared purpose, and a deep commitment to collaboration. Regular briefings and feedback loops ensure alignment, while open communication and psychological safety allow frontline workers to voice concerns and adapt strategies in real

time. Despite the chaos of disaster zones, WCK maintains a culture of trust, respect, and agility. Their success in logistics is driven by the way they lead through empathy, clarity, and collective accountability. In moments of crisis, they model what resilient, purpose-driven teamwork looks like.[1]

As leaders, we must recognise that team dynamics are not a luxury; they are a strategic imperative. Today more than ever where agility and collaboration replace rigid hierarchies, the way teams interact is equally as critical as what they produce. I often share with my clients that if we're not intentionally shaping team dynamics, we're not leading. Instead, we are simply managing. Management alone doesn't unlock the full potential of our teams. But when we connect and reciprocally support and grow one another, we unleash a powerhouse of innovation and productivity.

When working with a nonprofit, I guided them through a process of developing their healthy team dynamics to encompass the interpersonal and structural forces that shape how individuals communicate, collaborate, and perform. Over a period of four months, we reviewed, renewed and regenerated

---

1   World Central Kitchen. (n.d.). *World Central Kitchen.* https://wck. org/ This is the main website. World Central Kitchen. (n.d.). Mission, vision & values. https://wck.org/mission-vision-values

key team dynamic concepts such as trust, role clarity, psychological safety, conflict resolution, and shared purpose. According to McKinsey's Organizational Health Index,[2] high-performing teams are groups of skilled individuals who are also systems of interaction where behaviours like alignment, trust, and decision-making drive outcomes. As leaders, our role is to cultivate these systems deliberately, lifting others by creating environments where they can thrive.

Healthy team dynamics are shaped by four foundational dimensions: configuration, aligned goals and commitment, psychological safety, and accountability and clarity.

One of the most critical dimensions is configuration where the clarity of roles intersects with the diversity of perspectives. Role clarity reduces confusion and overlap, while cognitive diversity fuels innovation and adaptability. But diversity alone is not the lever for performance. Evidence shows that task knowledge diversity only enhances outcomes when role clarity and implicit coordination are high.[3] Structure, then, is what activates the power of difference.

---

2 McKinsey & Company. (2024, February 12). The power of organizational health. McKinsey and Company. https://www.mckinsey.com/capabilities/people-and-organizational-performance/our-insights/organizational-health-is-still-the-key-to-long-term-performance

3 Chen, S., Wang, W., Cheng, J., & Teng, D. (2021). Activating the benefit of diversity through team role clarity and implicit coordination. *Small Group Research*, 52(4), 379–404. https://doi.org/10.1177/1046496420958131

The second dimension of healthy team dynamics is the alignment between shared goals and collective commitment. When teams are united around a clear mission, they move faster, decide smarter, and stay engaged. Pawliw[4] observes that teams willing to take interpersonal risks such as naming inconvenient truths or challenging assumptions are more innovative and resilient. This is where leadership becomes transformational. Why? Because transformational leadership connects conflict resolution to shared values. When we focus on shared values, we invite teams to navigate disagreement with purpose and grace.

Psychological safety is the third foundational dimension in healthy team dynamics. We can learn from Google's Project Aristotle. In their research, they noted that teams that feel safe to speak up, admit mistakes, and offer new ideas consistently outperform others.[5] Project Aristotle emphasises that conversation turns and ostentatious listening are critical to encourage employee voice. As covered in Chapter 8, conflict intelligence, psychological safety fosters open communication and trust. When there is poor communication and no basis for trust, individuals

---

4 Pawliw, J. P. (2025, September 4). The secret to building a high-performing team. Harvard Business Review. https://hbr.org/2025/09/the-secret-to-building-a-high-performing-team

5 Google re: Work. (n.d.). Guide: Understand team effectiveness. https://rework.withgoogle.com/intl/en/guides/understanding-team-effectiveness

are psychologically unsafe, which means they do not turn up to work as their best self. The organisational implications for this poor attitude are lack of engagement resulting in low interaction, productivity and innovation, to name a few. Leaders who model vulnerability and curiosity lift others by making it safe to learn, fail, and grow.[6]

Another consideration of effective and healthy team dynamics is accountability and clarity. When expectations are clear and team members follow through, dependability becomes a norm. Dependability builds trust and reinforces a culture of excellence.[7] Dependability and accountability are about facilitating empowerment, and not about control. Leaders who set clear expectations and revisit them regularly create space for autonomy and ownership.

The four core dimensions for healthy team dynamics don't operate in isolation but reinforce one another when invested in as part of a strategy. When leaders intentionally cultivate them, they create environments where healthy conflict thrives, voices are valued, and performance is elevated. This is the essence of transformational leadership: lifting others by shaping the conditions for collective success. The

---

6   Clark, T. R. (2020). *The 4 stages of psychological safety: Defining the path to inclusion and innovation.* Berrett-Koehler Publishers.
7   Lencioni, P. M. (2002). *The five dysfunctions of a team: A leadership fable.* Jossey-Bass.

Belonging and Performance Matrix[8] shown in Figure 9.1 is an example of navigating team dynamics. As leaders, we have the power and responsibility to shape these conditions for our teams.

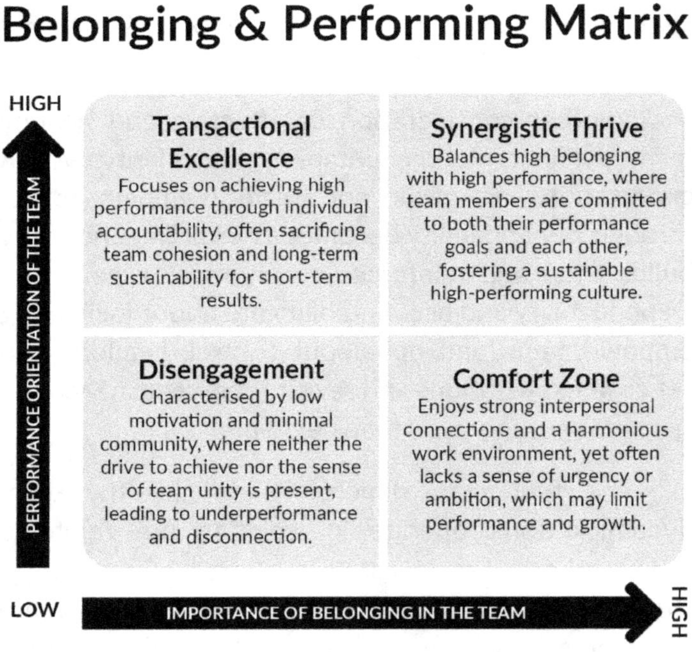

Belonging & Performing Matrix

Figure 9.1: Source: Coetzee, Pleinert & Hoch (2024), The dynamics of belonging.[8]

---

8 Coetzee, D., Pleinert, H., & Hoch, D. (2024). The dynamics of belonging: A quadrant-based analysis of team cohesion and performance. https://www.researchgate.net/publication/381112049_The_Dynamics_of_Belonging_A_Quadrant-Based_Analysis_of_Team_Cohesion_and_Performance

The Belonging and Performance Matrix uses two critical dimensions, sense of belonging and performance outcomes, to categorise team dynamics. Consider the examples provided.

Low Belonging / Low Performance
Teams in this quadrant often suffer from disengagement, unclear roles, and poor communication.

In a large healthcare organisation, a cross-functional team was tasked with implementing a new IT system. Due to lack of onboarding and unclear leadership, team members felt isolated and confused about their responsibilities. The project stalled, and several members requested reassignment.

High Belonging / Low Performance
While team members feel connected, lack of clarity or accountability may hinder results.

A fundraising committee in a nonprofit had strong camaraderie but failed to meet its annual targets. Members hesitated to hold one another accountable because they prioritised committee harmony over results. Eventually, leadership had to intervene to reset expectations and introduce clearer processes.

Low Belonging / High Performance
These teams might deliver results but often at the cost of burnout, turnover, or conflict.

In a global consulting firm, a high-performing team delivered exceptional client outcomes but experienced high turnover. Exit interviews revealed that members felt unsupported and disconnected, leading to stress and eventual burnout.

High Belonging / High Performance
The ideal quadrant, where psychological safety, trust, and shared goals drive sustainable success.

At a local primary school, the Year 6 teaching team was recognised for both outstanding student outcomes and a positive staff culture. The principal noted that the team's high trust and open communication allowed them to adapt quickly to curriculum changes and support one another through personal and professional challenges. Staff surveys revealed that teachers felt valued, supported, and empowered to innovate. As a result, student engagement and achievement were consistently above average, and staff turnover in the team was virtually non-existent.

The belonging and performance framework, a cornerstone of our discussion, is rooted in qualitative research across corporate, educational, sports, and public sectors. It underscores belonging as a potent driver of performance; belonging is not merely a feel-good factor. Teams that foster both emotional connection and operational clarity are certainly more resilient, innovative, and effective but, more so, are better equipped to navigate the complexities of the modern workplace.

PAUSE AND REFLECT

Consider the Belonging and Performance Matrix on page 186.

- Where would you rate the team dynamics of the team you currently lead or of which you are a part? This exercise involves an assessment of your team's performance and ownership of your team's dynamics.

- What do you need to do more of or less of, given your reflection? Your insights and actions are crucial in shaping your team's future.

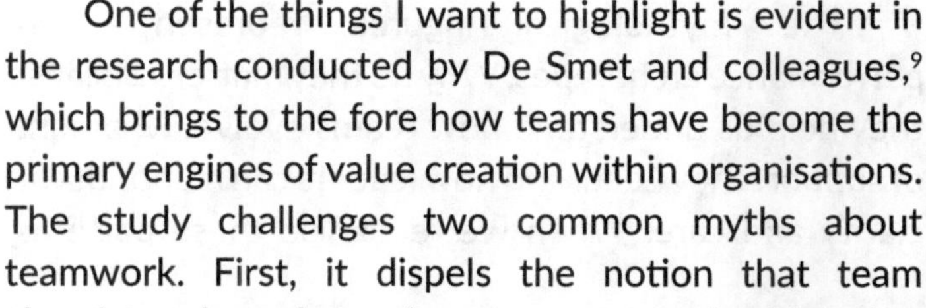

One of the things I want to highlight is evident in the research conducted by De Smet and colleagues,[9] which brings to the fore how teams have become the primary engines of value creation within organisations. The study challenges two common myths about teamwork. First, it dispels the notion that team chemistry alone determines success, emphasising that

---

9 De Smet, A., D'Auria, G., Albaharna, M., & coauthors. (2025, September 3). Team building for a new era. McKinsey and Company. https://www.mckinsey.com/featured-insights/mckinsey-guide-to-navigating-the-new-world-of-work/team-building-for-a-new-era

effective teams are not simply the result of members naturally *clicking* or getting on well. Second, it refutes the idea that a single, heroic leader can guarantee team performance. The study highlights the significance of structural and contextual factors, such as trust and open communication, in shaping team outcomes.

Team performance archetypes, shown in Figure 9.2, is a framework that encourages leaders to move beyond static models of team development and instead recognise that teams may shift between archetypes as they respond to internal and external challenges.[10] Let's simplify what researchers discovered about how teams perform over time. They reviewed a decade's worth of studies and found that teams tend to follow one of five distinct performance patterns. To make these patterns memorable, they named them after mythological Greek and Roman figures: Jupiter, Neptune, Pluto, Icarus, and Odysseus.

The mythological figures represent team performance archetypes. Why do they matter? Because they help us understand how teams evolve, what kind of support they need, and how leaders can respond with clarity and care. When we recognise these patterns,

---

10 Quigley, N. R., Collins, C. G., Gibson, C. B., & Parker, S. K. (2018). Team performance archetypes: Toward a new conceptualization of team performance over time. *Group & Organization Management*, 43(5), 787–824. https://doi.org/10.1177/1059601118794344

we can lead with intention – supporting growth, addressing challenges, and celebrating progress.

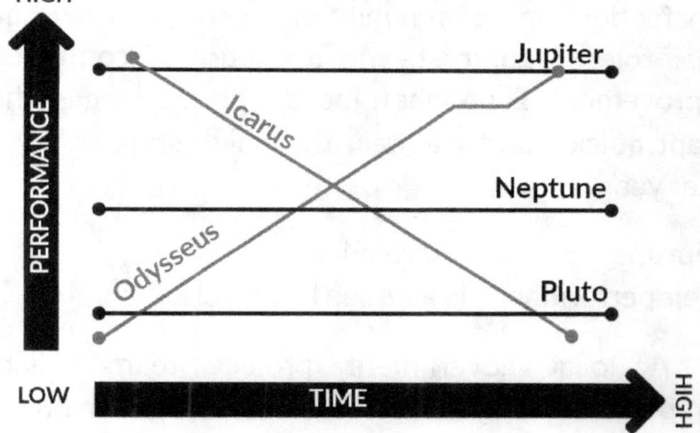

Figure 9.2: Source: N. Bonfiglio-Pavisich, © (2025). (Derived from: Quigley et al. (2018), Team performance archetypes.[10])

This framework is a practical tool for anyone who leads, supports, or works within teams. It reminds us that performance isn't fixed. It's a journey. With the right insight and action, every team has the potential to grow. Teams are adaptable and flexible for leaders who like to lift as they lead, allowing them to target interventions that lead to the maturation of team dynamics. I've used this model and found it can be applied across different sectors.

Jupiter – the high flyers

These teams consistently perform at a top level.

A school's senior leadership team has worked together for several years, consistently achieving outstanding results in student outcomes, staff satisfaction, and community engagement. They have clear roles, high trust, and a culture of continuous improvement. Even when faced with challenges, they adapt quickly and maintain their high standards year after year.

Neptune – steady and reliable.

Their performance is average but stable.

A local government project team reliably completes its assigned tasks on time and within budget but rarely exceeds expectations or innovates. The team members get along well and follow established procedures, but there is little drive to push beyond the status quo. However, with the right leadership strategies, this stable and predictable performance can be transformed into exceptional performance, instilling a sense of hope in leaders.

Pluto – struggling teams.

They consistently under-perform and need support.

A retail store's sales team has struggled for several quarters, consistently missing targets and experiencing high turnover. Communication is poor, morale is low, and there is little accountability. Despite management interventions, the team remains stuck in a cycle of underperformance.

Icarus – the fast starters.
They begin strong but lose momentum and decline.

A start-up's founding team launches with great enthusiasm and quickly achieves early success, attracting media attention and investment. However, as the company grows, internal conflicts and unclear roles emerge. The team's performance drops sharply, and several key members leave, causing momentum to stall.

Odysseus – the late bloomers.
They start slow but grow stronger over time.

A newly-formed school improvement committee initially struggles with unclear goals and a lack of cohesion. Over time, with strong leadership and targeted professional development, the team builds trust, clarifies roles, and implements effective strategies. Their performance steadily improves, and they eventually become a model for other committees in the district.

While the Team Performance Archetype Framework provides different approaches to understanding team dynamics, these archetypes are not fixed. Why? The archetypes are effectual and influenced by factors such as leadership style, team composition, and organisational culture. Delice and colleagues,[11] highlight the importance of measuring team dynamics over time, noting that emergent states, like trust, cohesion, and shared cognition, can shift as teams encounter new challenges or opportunities. Leaders can better understand and influence the evolution of their teams and ultimately support sustained high performance by adopting a longitudinal perspective and leveraging methodological tools such as agent-based simulations and growth modelling.

What can you do as a leader who seeks to lift others?

Research by Oyefusi[12] underscores the pivotal role that leaders play in shaping team dynamics and team productivity. Leaders are responsible for setting strategic direction as well as cultivating the behavioural norms that guide how team members interact. Leadership behaviour and personality are instrumental in communicating organisational values and establishing the expectations that underpin

---

11 Delice, F., Rousseau, M., & Feitosa, J. (2019). Advancing teams research: What, when, and how to measure team dynamics over time. *Frontiers in Psychology*, 10, Article 1324. https://doi.org/10.3389/fpsyg.2019.01324

12 Oyefusi, F. (2022). Team and group dynamics in organizations: Effect on productivity and performance. *Journal of Human Resource and Sustainability Studies*, 10(1), 111–122. https://doi.org/10.4236/jhrss.2022.101008

effective teamwork. Essentially, this means leaders need to practise what they preach.

Leaders cannot expect their employees to behave in one way and them in another. When leaders are intentional about modelling positive behaviours and reinforcing shared norms, they create an environment where collaboration and motivation can flourish. For example, Coldplay's kiss cam moment at a concert in New York in 2025 innocently exposed Astronomer CEO Andy Byron and the Chief Human Resources Officer, Kristin Cabot. Both individuals resigned because of the fallout, implications for their careers, workplace ethics, and their marriages.[13]

Leaders who seek to lift others as they lead must not forget the impact of leadership on new team members. Liao, Zhou and Yin[14] investigated the impact of organisational socialisation on team innovation performance, focusing on the role of leadership. Their cross-level model, published in *Psychology Research and Behavior Management*, demonstrated that, when leaders actively support new employees through clear communication of organisational norms, values, and

---

13 O'Neill, N. (2025, July 17). Astronomer CEO Andy Byron gushed about Kristin Cabot's hiring—months before getting caught on Coldplay's kiss cam. *New York Post*. https://nypost.com/2025/07/17/us-news

14 Liao, G., Zhou, J., & Yin, J. (2022). Effect of organizational socialization of new employees on team innovation performance: A cross-level model. *Psychology Research and Behavior Management*, 15, 1017–1031. https://doi.org/10.2147/PRBM.S359773

expectations, newcomers are more likely to engage in positive behaviours such as knowledge sharing and voice (speaking up with ideas or concerns). These findings are also reflected in the work of Dai and Fang[15] who argue that leaders who live and breathe the organisational values enable newcomers to integrate more smoothly into their respective teams and or organisations. The research makes it clear that leadership cannot be a passive function; it has to be an active force in shaping the social fabric of teams. By prioritising the development and reinforcement of constructive team norms, leaders can unlock higher levels of engagement, innovation, and productivity.

Leaders who truly lift others understand that their influence will shape both team performance and the culture and well-being of every member. To lead with impact, I encourage leaders to embrace three essential mantras: **be present, not passive** (actively engage with your team and listen deeply to their needs); **be generous, not jealous** (celebrate the successes of others and share opportunities for growth); and **be intentional, not incidental** (set clear expectations and model the values you wish to see). By living these mantras, leaders foster trust, psychological safety, and a sense of belonging, and the fostering of these

---

15 Dai, X., & Fang, Y. (2023). Does inclusive leadership affect the organizational socialization of newcomers from diverse backgrounds? The mediating role of psychological capital. *Frontiers in Psychology*, 14, Article 1138101. https://doi.org/10.3389/fpsyg.2023.1138101

qualities empowers teams to collaborate, innovate, and thrive together. Ultimately, leadership is about creating an environment where everyone is valued and inspired to contribute their best.

• • •

Takeaways

- Leadership shapes team culture.

- Team archetypes evolve.

- Integration of new members matters.

- Clear norms drive productivity.

- Continuous development is essential.

What will you START doing?

What will you CONTINUE doing?

What will you STOP doing?

Chapter Ten

Recognition and Reward – Lifting Others to Lead

Leaders have a responsibility to open doors and create opportunities for others and to support them to reach their full potential. ~ Dr Anne Poelina

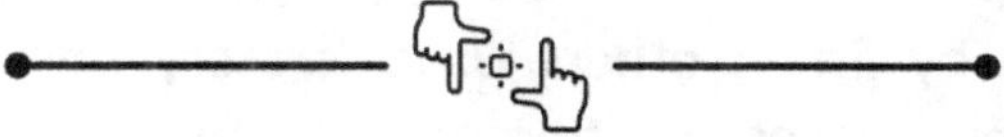

Jason showed up to work every day early, prepared, committed. For two years, he poured his energy into the company, solving problems, driving projects, and quietly holding the weight of success on his shoulders. However, under the leadership of an autocratic CEO who claimed every win as their own, his contributions went largely unnoticed. No acknowledgement. No voice. No seat at the table. Over time, the silence eroded his spirit. His output

declined, not from lack of skill, but from a growing sense that he did not matter.

Then something remarkable happened. The board, sensing the toxic undercurrent, made a bold decision to replace the CEO. The new leader, with a people-first approach, acknowledged Jason for the first time in a long time. He was invited to meetings, and his insights were sought. Moreover, the impact was profound: Jason's performance began to soar. Not because he was given permission, but because he was finally given recognition. He showed up with energy, with ideas, and with a renewed sense of purpose.

The Essence of Recognition and Reward

At the core of leadership is a simple yet profound truth: we rise by lifting others. Jason's story reveals that leadership makes a difference. When we recognise people, we not only improve performance we also restore belief and inspire brilliance. Recognition and reward are declarations of belief that say, "I see you, I value you, I believe in what you bring". When leaders take the time to recognise, affirm and reward meaningfully, they cultivate cultures of belonging, trust, and shared purpose. This is how we build communities where people do more than work – they thrive.

What Do Recognition and Reward Really Mean?

Recognition is described as the intentional acknowledgement of someone's effort, behaviour, or achievement. It can be quiet or loud, formal or spontaneous, but it must be sincere by being aligned with who we are and what we stand for. Recognition is not a throwaway "Good job!" in passing. That kind of comment, while well-intentioned, often leaves the recipient wondering: What was good about it? Why does it matter? As leaders, we need to be intentional. Recognition should be specific, values-based, and connected to impact.[1]

In the context of workplace leadership, reward is the tangible expression of appreciation whether it's through bonuses, promotions, gifts, or other forms of recognition. These gestures signal to individuals that their contributions are valued and impactful. However, it's essential that all reward practices are aligned with legislative requirements, organisational policies, and professional codes of conduct. When recognition is both meaningful and compliant, it not only reinforces performance but also strengthens trust and integrity within the team culture. However, let us be clear:

---

1 Tetrick, L. E., & Haimann, C. R. (2014). Employee recognition. In A. Day, E. K. Kelloway, & J. J. Hurrell, Jr. (Eds.), *Workplace well-being: How to build psychologically healthy workplaces* (pp. 161–174). Wiley Blackwell. https://doi.org/10.1002/9781118469392.ch8

reward without recognition is hollow. It is the meaning behind the gesture that makes it powerful.[2]

What Does Recognition Look and Sound Like?

Behavioural science tells us that recognition is a natural reinforcer. Recognition has outcome utility which means that it both feels good and provides benefits. It drives performance, confidence, and retention. When people are seen, they show up differently, and they lead differently.[3] Meisha Ann Martin, Senior Director of People and Analytics Research at Workhuman, in collaboration with Gallup, tracked over 3,400 employees between 2022 and 2024.[4] Her findings

---

2 Nelson, B. (2016). You get what you reward: A research-based approach to employee recognition. In M. J. Grawitch & D. W. Ballard (Eds.), *The psychologically healthy workplace: Building a win-win environment for organizations and employees* (pp. 157–179). American Psychological Association. https://doi.org/10.1037/14731-008

3 O'Flaherty, S., Sanders, M. T., & Whillans, A. (2021). Research: A little recognition can provide a big morale boost. *Harvard Business Review.* https://hbr.org/2021/03/research-a-little-recognition-can-provide-a-big-morale-boost

4 Martin, M. A., & Gallup. (2024, September 18). New Workhuman and Gallup research finds recognition in the workplace could prevent 45% of voluntary turnover. *Business Wire.* https://www.businesswire.com/news/home/20240918942631/en/New-Workhuman-and-Gallup-Research-Finds-Recognition-in-the-Workplace-Could-Prevent-45-of-Voluntary-Turnover

were clear: employees who were regularly recognised were 45 percent less likely to leave their jobs. They showed higher self-esteem, greater confidence, and a stronger sense of purpose.

The literature on the role of recognition and reward in the workplace highlights the significant shifts in behaviour that occur when employees are valued. I believe that recognition and reward provide the soil in which productivity and loyalty grow. Christopher Littlefield, a contributor to Harvard Business Review, has written about what happens when employees are recognised for the work they do.[5] He highlights a 40 percent increase in employee engagement that is reflective of communication, trust, and goodwill. Likewise, Luthans and Stajkovic[6] among other researchers, remind us that non-financial recognition – a heartfelt thank you, public praise, meaningful feedback – can improve performance by 30 percent to 41 percent. That is more than mere data: that is impact.

---

5   Littlefield, C. (2022). A better way to recognize your employees. *Harvard Business Review*. https://hbr.org/2022/10/a-better-way-to-recognize-your-employees

6   Luthans, F., & Stajkovic, A. D. (2006). The impact of recognition on employee performance: Theory, research and practice. Retrieved October 10.

Types of Recognition in the Workplace

Recognition is a spectrum from informal moments to formal ceremonies. Broadly speaking, we can identify the following forms:

- **Personal Recognition** – A handwritten note, a quiet thank you, a moment of connection.

- **Peer-to-Peer Recognition** – Encouraging team members to lift one another.

- **Manager-Led Recognition** – Structured, intentional, and tied to values.

- **Organisational Recognition** – Company-wide acknowledgements that reinforce culture.

When applied to real-life situations, these forms of recognition might look slightly different because of the context but still have the same outcomes. Figure 10.1 illustrates the ways recognition and reward were framed in an organisation with which I worked. For the purposes of this example, we'll refer to the company as McIntyre.

Four Types of Recognition and Reward

Informal Recognition	**Formal Recognition**
Social Recognition	**Values-Based Recognition**

Figure 10.1: Source: N. Bonfiglio-Pavisich, ©
(2025).

Informal Recognition

A simple thank you, shout-out in a meeting, or a handwritten note.

In McIntyre's Learning and Development team, informal recognition is seamlessly integrated into the everyday work rhythm. A handwritten note left on a desk after a successful training session, or a spontaneous shout-out during a morning huddle, reminds employees that their efforts are seen. Similarly, in the marketing department, a simple thank-you email after a successful campaign or a shout-out during a team meeting can have the same effect. These gestures may be small, but they carry weight. They say, "I noticed, I appreciate you". And when people are appreciated in the moment, they show up with more heart the next time.

Formal Recognition

Structured programs like Employee of the Month, service awards, or peer-nominated accolades.

McIntyre runs a structured Employee of the Month program in one of the organisation's departments. Nominations are submitted by peers, families, and managers, and winners are recognised with certificates, vouchers, and a feature in the internal newsletter. Importantly, the significance of the award and each recognition is tied to a specific act of care, creativity or leadership. In other words, the recognition is no longer a single act but becomes a part of a story and a rhythm of appreciation that reinforces excellence and builds a culture where achievement is celebrated, not assumed.

Social Recognition

Public praise on internal platforms or social media.

McIntyre's communications team amplifies recognition through public platforms. Staff achievements are regularly shared on the organisation's social media channels, celebrating everything from fundraising milestones to acts of kindness. One support worker was featured for organising a community garden project with residents. Her story reached hundreds and inspired others across the sector validated the individual, strengthened the collective identity of the organisation and also invited the wider community into the celebration. It greatly enhanced the organisation's reputation as a socially responsible and caring entity, which can attract more talent and customers.

Values-Based Recognition
Tied to organisational values, reinforcing behaviours that align with the company's mission.

Recognition in McIntyre's outreach and inclusion team is deeply tied to the organisation's core values of kindness, creativity, and person-centred support. Staff are acknowledged both for what they do and for how they do it. For example, a team member who advocated tirelessly for a person's right to choose their own support plan was recognised in the form of a values award presented at the annual conference with a story that highlighted her alignment with McIntyre's mission. This kind of recognition reinforces the behaviours that matter most and reminds everyone why they do the work they do.

McIntyre and I co-designed a recognition framework that reflects the heart of leadership: lifting others to lead. Recognition, when done well, becomes a strategic gesture that builds cultures of belonging, trust, and shared purpose. The four distinct types of recognition developed at McIntyre were aligned across departments to ensure consistency in delivery and impact. Transparency was a cornerstone of this framework. Every recognition moment, whether quiet or public, was tied to values that were clearly communicated and intentionally designed to elevate both the individual and the collective. This framework recognised effort, of course, but it's purpose was to build momentum. People now had a reason to show up, speak up, and lead from where they were. That's the power of recognition when it's done with heart, clarity, and purpose.

PAUSE AND REFLECT

- What recognition practices exist in your organisation?

- What work needs to be done to enable the organisation to align those recognition practices with company values and productivity in the workplace?

Positive Impact

A review by the Chartered Institute of Personnel and Development[7] revealed that employee recognition and non-financial rewards have a significant and generally positive impact on workplace performance. The Institute noted that high-quality studies, including randomised controlled trials, consistently highlighted moderate to significant improvements in productivity because of recognition, whether through verbal praise, thank-you cards, or symbolic gestures.

Brené Brown in her book, *Dare to Lead*,[8] emphasised that authentic recognition of employees created a platform of trust and a culture where they are seen, heard, and valued. These forms of recognition also enhanced intrinsic motivation, with employees demonstrating greater interest and enjoyment in their work compared with those who receive financial rewards or none at all. Furthermore, recognition programs have been shown to reduce absenteeism and generate positive spillover effects within teams, especially when the recognised individual holds a central role. Positive spillover effects refer to the beneficial impact of recognition on the morale, motivation, and performance of other team members,

---

7   Barends, E., Wietrak, E., Cioca, I., & Rousseau, D. (2022). Employee recognition and non-financial rewards: An evidence review. Scientific summary. London: Chartered Institute of Personnel and Development.
8   Brown, B. (2018). *Dare to lead.* Vermilion.

creating a ripple effect of improved engagement and productivity.

However, it is worth noting that research in the area of recognition and rewards consistently finds that recognition must be applied thoughtfully. When recognition is given merely for completing tasks without regard to performance standards, it can actually diminish motivation and effectiveness. Additionally, public recognition may sometimes cause envy or discomfort among peers, potentially undermining team cohesion and the intrinsic motivation of high performers. To avoid such pitfalls, leaders can maintain fairness and transparency in the distribution of recognition. For instance, they can establish clear criteria for recognition, ensure that all team members have equal opportunities to be recognised, and provide feedback on why specific individuals are being recognised.

It's also important to consider individual factors that influence the effectiveness of recognition. Bear in mind that recognition has a more substantial impact when employees perceive their work as less meaningful, suggesting it can serve as a compensatory motivator. It highlights the importance of leaders being attentive and considerate of their employees' individual needs when designing recognition programs.

Although recognition speaks to the heart, reward often speaks to the tangible value of contribution.

Reward

Rewards in the workplace play a vital role in shaping employee behaviour, enhancing productivity, and reducing attrition.[9] Unlike recognition, which is often intangible and relational, rewards are typically tangible, transactional, and expected.[10] These reward categories include, but are not limited to, promotions, development opportunities, flexible work arrangements, and symbolic items such as thank-you cards or small gifts, which go a long way to increasing employee motivation.

However, tangible, transactional, and expected rewards are best applied with the types of recognition shown in Figure 10.2. Leaders who decided on the recognition described in the examples in the subsequent pages, gave more than rewards: they gave employees a reason for taking greater interest and enjoyment in their work, which translates into improved performance outcomes and improved employee morale and job satisfaction.

---

9 Antoni, C. H., Baeten, X., Perkins, S. J., Shaw, J. D., & Vartiainen, M. (2017). Reward management: Linking employee motivation and organizational performance [Editorial]. *Journal of Personnel Psychology*, 16(2), 57–60. https://doi.org/10.1027/1866-5888/a000187

10 Figueiredo, E., Margaça, C., Sánchez García, J. C., & Ribeiro, C. (2025). The contribution of reward systems in the work context: A systematic review of the literature and directions for future research. *Journal of the Knowledge Economy*. https://doi.org/10.1007/s13132-024-02492-w

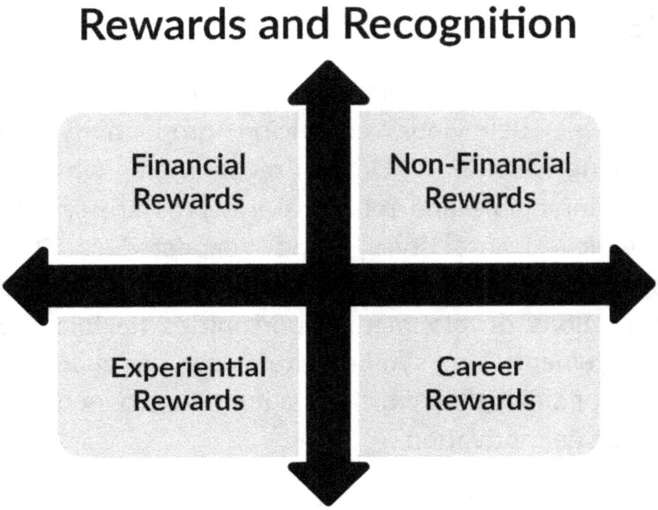

Rewards and Recognition

Figure 10.2: Source: N. Bonfiglio-Pavisich, © (2025).

Financial Rewards

Bonuses, wage increases, raises, and stock options.

Financial rewards, such as bonuses, salary increases, and stock options, are among the most direct and measurable forms of employee incentives because they signal the economic value of employees, provide immediate gratification, and reinforce goal-oriented behaviour. Bonuses, often tied to performance metrics or company profitability, are an immediate form of recognition and appreciation, whereas salary increases or raises signify long-term appreciation and career progression. Stock options, on the other hand, align employee interests with the company's financial success, encouraging a sense of ownership and commitment. These rewards are particularly effective in attracting and retaining talent, especially in competitive industries, and they serve as strong motivators for productivity when transparently linked to performance outcomes. [11]

Nurses at a regional hospital in Victoria who consistently exceed patient care benchmarks are awarded quarterly bonuses, not for financial compensation but to acknowledge personal achievement, to say "Your excellence matters, your impact is seen". When leaders tie financial rewards to outcomes that reflect care and quality, they reinforce the behaviours that save lives and build trust, making the recipients experience being deeply valued and recognised.

Non-Financial Rewards
Extra time off, flexible work arrangements, and professional development opportunities.

Non-financial, experiential, and career rewards are nuanced benefits that contribute to employee satisfaction and long-term engagement. Non-financial rewards such as extra time off, flexible work arrangements, and professional development opportunities support work-life balance and personal growth, which are increasingly valued in modern

---

11 Simon Sinek. (2022, September). What are we rewarding? [YouTube Video].

workplaces. When thoughtfully designed and aligned with performance standards, non-financial rewards can serve as powerful motivators, reinforcing desired behaviours and encouraging sustained effort.[12]

Teachers in a public school district in Queensland are offered flexible work arrangements and professional development scholarships. These non-financial rewards recognise the emotional labour and intellectual investment educators make daily, making their experience understood and appreciated. A teacher who leads a successful literacy initiative might be given extra planning time or access to a leadership development course. These gestures say, "We believe in your growth, and we are committed to your long-term success". When people invested in, they invest back.

Experiential Rewards
Team retreats, lunch with leadership, and travel incentives.

Experiential rewards, such as team retreats, lunches with leadership, or travel incentives, create memorable experiences that enhance connection, recognition, and a sense of belonging.

At a boutique hotel chain in New South Wales, top-performing staff are invited to annual team retreats in scenic locations. One concierge, known for

---

12 Pink, D. H. (2024). Drive: *The surprising truth about what motivates us* (Updated ed.). Riverhead Books.

consistently going above and beyond for guests, was rewarded with a weekend retreat and lunch with the executive team. These experiential rewards create memories, deepen relationships, and say, "You're part of something bigger". They transform recognition into connection.

Career Rewards
Promotions, stretch assignments, and mentorship opportunities.

Career rewards, including promotions, stretch assignments, and mentorship, signal investment in an employee's future and help build loyalty by offering pathways for advancement. Together, these rewards enhance intrinsic motivation through powerful moments, reduce employee attrition, and cultivate a culture of appreciation and development.[13]

A local government office in Western Australia embeds career rewards into performance pathways. A project officer who led a successful community engagement initiative was offered a stretch assignment managing a cross-departmental task force. Later, she was paired with a senior mentor to prepare for a leadership role. These career rewards say, "We see your potential, let's grow it". And when leaders open doors, they build futures.

---

13 Shields, J., Rooney, J., Brown, M., & Kaine, S. (2025). *Managing employee performance and reward: Systems, practices and prospects* (3rd ed.). Cambridge University Press

PAUSE AND REFLECT

- What reward practices exist in your organisation?

- Are those practices fostering greater connection with company values and productivity in the workplace?

- Consider what work needs to be done to align these practices more closely with your company's values and goals.

Global Examples of Leaders Who Lift Through Recognition and Rewards

Satya Nadella (Microsoft)

Known for his empathetic leadership, Satya emphasises recognition as a tool for building inclusive cultures.[14] His approach to celebrating small wins and personal growth has transformed Microsoft's internal culture.

The mindset that Satya models and encourages forms the platform for curiosity, collaboration, and

---

14 Prakash, D., Bisla, M., & Rastogi, S. G. (2021). Understanding authentic leadership style: The Satya Nadella Microsoft approach. *Open Journal of Leadership*, 10(2), 95–109. https://doi.org/10.4236/ojl.2021.102007

continuous learning. These learning qualities are entrenched through opportunities for development and innovation. Satya's leadership style prioritises understanding and listening, empowering employees to express their ideas and take risks without fear of failure. His commitment to inclusivity ensures that diverse voices are heard and celebrated, creating a feedback-rich environment where recognition is both personal and collective, thereby fostering employee engagement and continuous improvement.

Indra Nooyi (Former CEO, PepsiCo)

Indra's strength in recognition is thanking the family members of staff for the quality rearing of their children.[15] She famously wrote personal letters to the parents of her senior executives, thanking them for raising such talented leaders. This intensely personal gesture created lasting loyalty and emotional connection. She has also encouraged social responsibility, sustainability, and employee well-being through her Performance with Purpose Strategy. Her 2+2+2 strategy encouraged the individual and professional development of senior executives to develop a holistic understanding and application of leadership: learning about 2 functions, 2 businesses, and 2 geographies.

---

15 Freeland, G. (2020, February 24). Indra Nooyi's passions: People, performance and purpose at PepsiCo and beyond. *Forbes.* https://www.forbes.com/sites/grantfreeland/2020/02/24/ indra-nooyis-passions-people-performance–purpose-at-pepsico-and-beyond/

Sir Richard Branson (Virgin Group)

Sir Richard is recognised for his diverse business interests and is well known for the way he acknowledges those who work for him. His brand of recognition focuses on the everyday interactions that occur in the workplace. He frequently calls employees to thank them, writes personal references, and makes a point to greet every individual when visiting Virgin offices.[16]

Sir Richard also emphasises peer-to-peer recognition, enabling employees to nominate one another based on Virgin's core values of innovation, customer service, community and the environment. With a focus on maintaining a culture of mutual respect, his inclusive approach fosters and inspires appreciation and autonomy, where employees are empowered and celebrated for their contributions. Branson says: "Take care of your employees and they'll take care of your business". His companies are known for providing generous rewards and a culture of celebration.[17]

---

16 Preston, J. (2017, April 20). Understanding the Richard Branson approach to leadership. *Virgin.* https://www.virgin.com/about-virgin/latest/understanding-richard-branson-approach-leadership

17 Schawbel, D. (2014, September 23). Richard Branson's three most important leadership principles. *Forbes.* https://www.forbes.com/sites/danschawbel/2014/09/23/richard-branson-his-3-most-important-leadership-principles/

Lifting Others to Lead: The Transformational Power

A key message I relay in my workshops for leaders is that our legacy is not defined solely by the goals we achieve; it's also defined by the people we elevate along the way. Recognition and reward, when thoughtfully and consistently applied, become instruments of transformation because they shape culture as well as enhance performance. Earlier in this chapter, I referred to an organisation that I named pseudonymously as McIntyre. In that project, we built a recognition framework rooted in transparency, alignment, and authenticity. So, we implemented a system with an embedded philosophy. We recognised effort along with outcomes. We rewarded growth, not perfection. We celebrated values as well as the metrics or outcomes that were driven by the values. From personal thank-you notes to peer-nominated accolades, from flexible work arrangements to career development pathways, every gesture was designed to affirm worth and inspire leadership.

When people are seen, they show up differently. They contribute with confidence, collaborate with purpose, and lead with heart. Recognition and reward, when done with intention, create ripple effects of belonging, initiative, and excellence. This is how leadership lifts others.

• • •

Takeaways

- Make recognition and rewards personal.

- Be timely in the distribution of recognition and rewards.

- Be specific and transparent about the criteria of recognition and rewards.

- Empower peer recognition.

What will you START doing?

What will you CONTINUE doing?

What will you STOP doing?

Conclusion

Leadership isn't a solo act. It's a shared experience, one that lives in the spaces between us, including you, the reader. It's not about titles, hierarchy, or authority. It's about how we show up, how we respond, and how we choose to lead with presence, purpose, and heart. In this third book of the *Show Up and Lead* series, we've explored what it truly means to lead in a way that lifts others. We've turned our attention outward to the teams we serve, the relationships we build, and the cultures we shape.

We began with trust, the bedrock of leadership. Trust is not given; it's earned through consistency, authenticity, and emotional presence. When we arrive with courage and clarity, we create environments where people, including you, the reader, feel safe to contribute, collaborate, and grow.

We then explored the difference between empowering and enabling. Leaders who lift others don't do the work for their teams; they equip them to do it themselves. Empowerment is the gift of belief, support, and opportunity.

We examined reality testing and social responsibility, two anchors that keep us grounded and accountable. Leadership is not solely focused on individual achievement; rather, it emphasises the significance of collective impact. It's about making decisions that benefit the whole, not the few.

We reflected on the balance between knowledge and experience, recognising that wisdom lives in both. Great leaders know when to speak and when to listen, when to guide and when to learn.

Communication, too, was a central theme and we recognised that our communication involves words plus how we listen, clarify, and respond.

We explored the power of healthy conflict, not as a disruption, but as a sign of engagement and growth. When conflict is handled with respect and emotional intelligence, it becomes a catalyst for growth.

We discussed team dynamics, recognition and rewards, because people, including you, need to be seen. We all need to know our work matters. Recognition isn't a luxury; it's a leadership imperative, and it's a way to show appreciation for your team's efforts.

And through it all, we returned to three guiding mantras:

- **Be present, not passive**

- **Be generous, not jealous**

- **Be intentional, not incidental**

These mantras are more than words. They are a call to action. They remind us that leadership is a daily practice; a choice to show up with integrity, to lift others with generosity, and to lead with intention. They challenge us to stay alert to how we present ourselves and the example we set. They invite us to reflect deeply on how others experience us and how, through our presence, we empower them to experience themselves differently.

So, as you close this book, I invite you to pause, to reflect and to recommit:

- Are you showing up with presence in the spaces that matter most?

- Are you leading with generosity, creating room for others to rise?

- Are you making intentional choices that align with your values and vision?

Leadership that lifts others is a way of being, not a destination. It's how we show up in every conversation, every decision, every moment. Leadership that lifts others is how we leave people feeling after they've worked with us. Most significantly, it's how we build something that lasts beyond results to enduring relationships, resilience, and respect.

I hope this book becomes your companion, your mirror, and your map. Let it remind you that leadership is not about being the best in the room. Leadership is about helping others become their best because you were in the room.

Now, go! Lead. Lift. Show up.

**Other books in the Leadership Series
by Dr Nancy Bonfiglio-Pavisich**

For Further Reading

Alzaabi, H. S. M. A., & Dilawer, T. (2023). The importance of trust in leadership effectiveness. *International Journal of Research Publication and Reviews*, 4(7), 1788–1795. https://doi.org/10.55248/gengpi.4.723.17881795

Arunraj, R. I., Murugesan, P., Pandi, V., & Sivasubramanian, S. (2024). Effects of Employee Recognition Programs on Engagement and Retention. *Library of Progress-Library Science, Information Technology & Computer*, 44(3)

Boston Consulting Group. (2010, January 14). Indra K. Nooyi on Performance with Purpose. *BCG Publications*. https://www.bcg.com/publications/2010/indra-nooyi-performance-purpos

Brown, B. (2012). *Daring greatly: How the courage to be vulnerable transforms the way we live, love, parent, and lead.* Penguin Random House

Brown, B. (2017). *Braving the wilderness: The quest for true belonging and the courage to stand alone.* Vermilion

Clark, T. R. (2020). *The 4 stages of psychological safety: Defining the path to inclusion and innovation.* Berrett-Koehler Publishers.

Connor, J., & Hirani, K. (2020). *The Four Greatest Coaching Conversations.* Hachette UK.

Cote, C. (2023, August 24). Ethical leadership: Your social and ethical responsibilities. Harvard Business School Online. Retrieved from https://online.hbs.edu/blog/post/ethical-and-social-responsbility-in-business.

Du, S., Swaen, V., Lindgreen, A., & Sen, S. (2013). The roles of leadership styles in corporate social responsibility. *Journal of business ethics*, 114(1), 155-169.

Edmondson, A. C., and Bransby, D. P. (2023). Psychological safety comes of age: Observed themes in an established literature. *Annual Review of Organizational Psychology and Organizational Behavior*, 10, 55–78. https://doi.org/10.1146/annurev-orgpsych-120920-055217

Falconer, E. (2018). *How to Get Sh* t Done: Why Women Need to Stop Doing Everything So They Can Achieve Anything*. Simon and Schuster.

Gallup. https://www.prnewswire.com/news-releases/global-employee-engagement-drops-for-only-the-second-time-in-12-years-costing-the-worlds-economy-us438-billion-302434901.html (statistic reference)

Hansen, M. T. (2018). *Great at work: How top performers do less, work better, and achieve more.* Simon and Schuster.

Harter, J., & Pendell, R. (2025, April 23). *Global employee engagement drops for only the second time in 12 years, costing the world's economy US$438 billion.*

How to promote team trust and employee engagement How To Promote Team Trust And Employee Engagement By David Qu, Forbes Business Council June 09 2021. Former Forbes Councils Member. https://www.forbes.com/councils/forbesbusinesscouncil/2021/06/09/how-to-promote-team-trust-and-employee-engagement/

Kozlowski, S. W. J., & Ilgen, D. R. (2006). Enhancing the effectiveness of work groups and teams. *Psychological Science in the Public Interest*, 7(3), 77–124. https://doi.org/10.1111/j.1529-1006.2006.00030.x

MHR. (2019). Gaslighting widespread in the UK workplace. MHR.

Omeihe, I., Harrison, C., & Omeihe, K. (2021). Authentic leadership: A systematic literature review. *British Academy of Management Conference Proceedings*, 1–29. https://www.academia.edu/91114648/Authentic_Leadership_A_Systematic_Literature_Review

Rahim, M. A. (2011). *Managing conflict in organizations* (4th ed.). Transaction Publishers.

RSA. (2013, December 10). *Brené Brown on empathy* [Video]. YouTube. https://www.youtube.com/watch?v=1Evwgu369Jw.

Stajkovic, A. D., & Luthans, F. (1998). Self-efficacy and work-related performance: A meta-analysis. *Psychological Bulletin*, 124(2), 240–261. https://doi.org/10.1037/0033-2909.124.2.240

TeamDynamics. (2025, August 21). *The 5 behaviors of a cohesive team: A comprehensive guide for leaders.* The Table Group. https://www.teamdynamics.io/blog/the-5-behaviors-of-a-cohesive-team-a-comprehensive-guide-for-leaders

TEDx Talks You Tube June 2015 Claire McCarty Professor College of Business – Missing the obvious in employee recognition.

The Knowledge Academy. (n.d.). *What is social responsibility? Definition, types & examples.* Retrieved from https://www.theknowledgeacademy.com/blog/social-responsibility/

The Leadership Sphere. (2025, August 12). The impact of ethical leadership on society. Retrieved from https://theleadershipsphere.com.au/insights/the-impact-of-ethical-leadership-on-society/

Ting-Toomey, S. (2015). *Understanding intercultural communication* (2nd ed.). Oxford University Press.

Trust: The Key to an Engaged Workplace - Work Design Magazine by Christina Herrera and Susan Spiers 2021 work Design magazine. https://www.workdesign.com/2024/10/trust-the-key-to-an-engaged-workplace/